E M M A;

OR THE

FOUNDLING OF THE WOOD

A NOVEL.

BY

MISS BROOKE,

DAUGHTER OF THE LATE HENRY BROOKE, AUTHOR
OF THE FOOL OF QUALITY, ETC.

LONDON

PRINTED FOR J F HUGHES, 5, WIGMORE-STREET,
CAVINDISH-SQUARE,

By J. Swan, Angel Street, Newgate Street

AND SOLD BY B. CROSBY AND CO STATIONERS'-
COURT, LUDGATE-STREET,

1803,

PREFACE.

As it may appear strange that this little performance should remain so long unpublished after the death of Miss Brooke, it will be proper to state the reasons which have detained it from the public for such a length of time Miss Brooke, when dying, did not intimate to her friends any thing concerning this Novel , nor was it discovered till three or four years after, in a small trunk, which had lain unobserved by her surviving friends Upon opening the parcel, it was found to contain many other pieces and ma-

nuscripts, as well of our author as of
her father, the late Henry Brooke,
the well-known author of Gustavus
Vasa and the Fool of Quality. From
the irregular state in which it was
found, and the circumstance of her not
mentioning it to her friends, there is
reason to suppose, she considered it
as an unfinished production, not being able, from her sudden and fatal
indisposition, to give it the last hand
In transcribing the pages, we have not,
however, ventured to make many al-
terations, well knowing, that a spirited sketch must inevitably lose its
truth and originality, if retouched by
any pencil but that of the designer —
It is now ready for the perusal of the
public, and we are in hopes that the

little Foundling, as she has no better title to recommend her, will attract their attention, and meet with that favourable patronage, which all generous minds are ever ready to bestow on the orphan and unprotected

EMMA;

OR, THE

FOUNDLING OF THE WOOD.

In the fourth year of my infancy, I was left in the extensive wood of Hammond Castle, by a woman, who placed me under an old oak, where I cried myself asleep. Hunger, however, disturbed my repose, and, arising from my shady bower, I began to amuse myself with the flowers that bloomed in vast profusion around me. Looking wildly about, I beheld two ladies and a gentleman approach. I ran to them with open arms, and cried for bread. the gentleman took me up; 'you shall have bread, my dear,' said he.

B

'My mammy is gone away,' cried I 'Who is your mammy?' 'I don't know.' 'And what is your name, sweet child?' 'My name is Emma, Sir.'

He carried me to an ancient mansion, where I was fed and cherished I was soon reconciled to my new friends and situation, and became as blithe as the lamb on the plains.

There were two of the family who wanted to have me sent away, and disputes often arose, between them, about my continuance. The younger Miss Hammond and the elder brother, Lord George, wished to have me sent to nurse, but the rest of the family would not consent to part with me

Nature, it seems, had given me exterior grace, though fortune frowned on my birth. The infant ear is ever open to adulation, and all who saw me, praised my loveliness As I grew up, no pains were spared to instruct me in all useful accomplishments, and, before I attained my fifteenth year, I excelled in what few of my age could boast of Miss Hammond often sat in my apartment, and condescended to treat me with the familiarity of a sister. The younger daughter of this noble family was haughty pride was her ruling passion, and her amiable sister had no comfort in her society, so little were their minds in unison.

The disposition of the younger Mr Hammond was similar to that of his sister Charlotte As I grew up, he took a pleasure in instructing me, and putting such books into my hands as were best calculated to improve the mind.

His family spent the winter in the metropolis, but he seldom accompanied them, and his leisure hours were often devoted to me He was naturally of a pensive cast, and did not like the amusements of the town Often has he spent whole hours in my company, and when my governess praised me in his presence, it evidently gave him pleasure.

The winter was now approaching, and preparations making for the removal of the family to town; but a ball was to be given before their departure. Miss Hammond told me her mother intended I should be one of the party: I trembled at the idea, as I was seldom admitted into the presence of Lady Hammond. She was proud to excess, and the many good qualities she possessed were overbalanced by that one vice.

I was now at that age when a girl most stands in need of a mother, or some kind friend, to point out the path she should tread; but none such was doomed for Emma. I began to feel all the misery of my situation, though surrounded with splendor, and pined in secret for the knowledge of my parents.

The sweet ties of affinity are a cordial to the heart, and I felt myself alone in the world, though well protected the lovely Charlotte filled part of the vacuity in my bosom I was as fond of her as it was possible to be, and she returned a similar affection, which ended but with our lives.

Her brother Edwin, who loved her with the most sincere affection, was exactly of her own disposition, as I have before observed ; and, in this comparison, admit all the virtues a human heart is capable of possessing.

On the day before the ball, I happened to be walking alone in the garden, when Edwin approached me, and, with a look of fraternal solicitude, enquired why I seemed so pensive. ' You are now,' said he, ' Emma, arrived at that period when the eyes of man will behold you with delight believe not all sincere who praise you , it is their own gratification they have in view, when they throw out flattery as a bait; they will look on your situation in this family as an easy means of seduction, and suppose you will accept any offer to become independent. I understand you are going to town with the ladies, to launch, for the first time, into the great world, where you will find enemies under the semblance of friends Avoid the man who would in any degree tempt you to swerve from your duty, and the rules which I have laid down for your conduct.' I felt my obligations to this best of men, and told him, his advice to me should never be neglected; my heart was too full to say more.

Miss Hammond met me on my return to the house, and told me her mother desired my company to tea; a favour so seldom allowed, that I was surprised at her condescension.

I entered Lady Hammond's presence with a timidity I never could conquer. Her younger daughter, who was then in the room, cast on me a look of the most chilling disdain. 'Whom have we got here, pray?' said she. 'So, Miss Emma, you are introduced to the parlour!' 'Why,' returned Lady Hammond, 'as Emma is a pretty, modest girl, I intend to have her sit with us sometimes' 'Indeed, ma'am,' said she, 'then I can tell you, I will not sit with such a girl, that no one knows. I am surprised at you, Lady Hammond! it was not enough for you to take her under your protection, but you must also make her one of the family! You are much fallen from your dignity, madam.' I was so abashed, that I could not find strength to leave the room.

The gentle Charlotte felt for my situation. I strove to rise, when the door opened, and Lord George made his appearance. He just deigned me a look of approbation ' Don't, Miss Emma, don't stir for my coming in.' ' Why, brother,' cried his sister, ' I wished she should: is she company for us, pray ?' ' My dear Harriet,' said he, ' you ought to comply with Lady Hammond's wishes, I suppose it was her desire that Emma should come to the parlour. Sit down, Miss Emma:' he handed me to a chair. His attention to me, during the evening, quite mortified the haughty spirit of his sister but I felt unhappy in her presence, and, at an early hour, withdrew to my apartment.

It plainly appeared, from what followed, that Lord George had that evening marked me for his prey, as I heard no more of my being permitted to go to the ball, and was happy, as I must have complied, if asked. At length the night came, when, all being engaged in revelling and dancing, Lord George entered my room. ' My lovely girl,' said he, ' I have just stolen from a scene, which your absence made insupportable, to assure you, that your image has so haunted me of late, that I can no longer refrain from declaring a passion, the most ardent and unconquerable. You are a captivating creature! and I love you even to dotage; if ye will consent to be mine, I will take you from the insolence of Harriet, and place you in a situation more suitable to such loveliness. You have it in your power to render me the happiest or most miserable of mankind.' He seemed intoxicated, and caught me in his arms: 'Begone, Sir!' I replied, almost sinking with terror. 'I'm amazed at your conduct: leave me instantly. Oh! will you deprive me of the only protection I have on earth!' 'I will protect my charming girl! I will provide you a residence! say you'll consent to live with me: you shall be your own mistress—I have a house and equipage at command, and my constant endeavours to please, will, in a short time, I hope, entitle me to your love.'

'Hold, my lord!' said I; 'consider what you are saying—I never will comply with any offers you can make contrary to virtue.'

The advice of his amiable brother came fresh to my mind at that instant.—' Leave me, my lord, and seek no farther the ruin of her who has no friend but in your own family. I feel all those obligations, nay, I am oppressed with them ; but, if you ever more renew your insulting offers, I will from that time quit this asylum of my youth.' My tears affected him, and he bid me good night; saying, as he went, ' Never again shall I cause you trouble, my charming girl!'

Lord George was a man not easily diverted from a favourite pursuit, and was firmly bent on seducing me, though he had promised to desist.

The following day I walked alone in the garden, and perceiving a folded paper on the walk, snatched it hastily up, and found it was a letter from my enemy to his friend, as follows.

Dear Ormsby,

You are a mere dunce, or you could not be at a loss for the cause of my stay in the country, when I have already told you of a bewitching little gipsey, that is grown up here—I have long had an eye on her, and am trying to get her consent to let me whip her off to town, where, you know, I can readily deceive my family as to her fate. Invention never forsook me on these occasions, but she is as coy as the d—l, and I fear will prove too cunning for me. You would be astonished at her answers to my addresses.—Where she has had all this experience, I cannot think, but strongly suspect that my brother has been tutoring her—he is very liberal of his advice to the fair, and would fain have every woman virtuous.—Faith, I believe, my dear fellow, he is better than either of us—pleasure has always been my deity and, while I have life, I must pay homage at the shrine of Venus.—Could I but get the charming Emma to add to the number of my favourites, I should style myself your happy and devoted

G. HAMMOND.

This letter too plainly proved what I had to fear. I stood riveted to the earth—a statue of woe. The first use I made of my returning reason, was to resolve to shew the letter to Miss Hammond; but again thought it would too much affect her gentle bosom to find, in her brother, so great a villain; the uneasiness it might occasion to her, retarded my purpose for that night, a circumstance which had nearly proved fatal to me.

Miss Hammond was seldom without objects for the exercise of her bounty; and, a family whom she had supported for nearly a year, having solicited some fresh attentions from her, she asked me to take a little money to them, and promised to come and meet me, on my return home. I could not refuse her commands, which were to me, at the time, a little alarming, after the fatal letter; but, recollecting that Lord George was gone out early in the morning, on a fishing party, I lulled my fears, and went to execute the orders of this best of women.

I found the poor father of the little family sitting on a bench, at the door of his cottage, and a female infant in his arms He rose, with a respectful look, on my approach There we e four children more, at a small fire, and the wretched mother on a bed of straw sick of an ague I gave her the money, and in exchange, I received a thousand blessings for her who sent it. My heart was grieved for the wretched family, there was something in them that interested— sweet sympathy of the human heart, which binds us to each other—I wished I could have staid longer, as I had often wished to hear their story The poor woman told me, if she recovered, she intended to beg, as she could no longer intrude on the bounty of an angel, as she called my friend ' Be ter days have I seen,' said she, ' ah' little do we know what misery may befal us '

I returned home, and crossing a stile, good heavens ' what was my surprise to find the hand of Lord George offered to assist me ' I almost fainted away ' Don't be so alarmed, Emma, I won't hurt you, my love.' ' Away, Sir ' I fear you more than death begone, I say, nor persecute me further. I never will comply with your wishes —Are there not women enough who will think you honour them by your attentions? Go, seek them, and leave a helpless orphan to enjoy her innocence' 'You make me miserable,' cried he 'it is true. I can find others not so cruel, yet not one whom I love like you.' 'Love!' said I, 'oh! name it not you are a stranger to its influence that sweet disinterested passion never existed in a libertine heart. But, perhaps, I misunderstand you, Sir, in that case, I ask your pardon, perhaps marriage is your intention. if so, I return you many thanks for your intended honour.'

At that instant I attempted to depart. I knew, though I gave him so well-merited a rebuke, his intentions were not honourable. 'If you consent to elope with me, lovely Emma,' said he, 'I will make you my wife in due time' He charged me to be secret, and never tell one of his family that he had any designs on me I begged he would detain me no longer, as I now found my strength reviving, which terror had nearly deprived me of.

I beheld Miss Hammond coming towards me, and my heart rejoiced at the sight, Lord George hid himself in an adjacent hedge. As we walked homeward, Miss Hammond told me I looked terrified 'What is the matter, I must know all that concerns my sweet girl?' 'With reluctance I will tell you,' said I. 'because it will give you sorrow.' 'I can guess it already, Emma did I not get a glimpse of my brother, as he passed, and concealed himself from me? I long feared what is now come to pass. knowing him to be an unprincipled libertine, who stops at nothing in the pursuit of his pleasures, yet, I hoped he was not so depraved as to attempt to seduce you, while under the protection of his mother'

I showed her the letter I had found, and told her all he had said to me. 'Emma,' said she, 'you must leave this house, something must be done immediately to withdraw the temptation from him But, Emma, tell me, has Edwin ever made any overtures to you? I own I once suspected him, but well knowing his amiable d-position, I grew

easy with regard to him on your account,
yet there was a certain confusion in his countenance, one day I caught him looking a
you '

'Edwin, madam, has been my best ad-
viser, he told me of the dark devices of his
own sex, and never in his life, paid me a
compliment ' I did justice to the virtues of
this amiable man—but could not tell her all
—on that I loved him too well for my peace,
that was too delicate a circumstance to be
disclosed I knew it not myself till too late
for recovery It stole imperceptibly on my
young heart, which was tremblingly alive to
friendship, gratitude, and affection Foolish, vain attachment' for what end, thought
I, should I indulge thee, but lasting misery!
I could not presume, or hope, for the prospect of being worthy of Mr Hammond's regard in any degree but compassion, yet,
even that hope flattered me he was interested, and had shown it on many occasions,
but nothing more. I felt for him all that
can be conceived of affection, esteem well
founded on his worth, and all the endearing

ties of the purest love it was more than
can be expressed by words   My heart had
yielded to the impression of his virtues   all
I myself possessed were of his own nurtur-
ing, and now the seeds of virtue he had placed flourished apace, but a rugged hand would
fain crop them ere they bloomed.—Cruel
wish!—I felt a secret shame in the consci-
ousness of loving Edwin oppressed with my
own inferiority, but he had, from nature,
all that was requisite to captivate the most
susceptible heart   a benign aspect, manly
form, and eyes expressive of love and sentiment. His brother was what most people
would style handsome , but his sensual soul
beamed in his eye, and a gloominess occasion-
ally overspread his face. His thoughts were
not always in a right train, and consequently
distorted his countenance, while the amiable and beloved Edwin shone forth with
all the sweetness of virtue. I often feared
that my feelings would betray me, as I frequently trembled and blushed at his sudden
approach.

Miss Hammond had consulted her mother

as to Lord George's conduct towards me, and they, well knowing his libertine principles fixed on a place to shelter the Orphan of the Wood from impending ruin. I was ordered to prepare in a few days, and we set out on a journey I knew not whither, attended only by a strange postillion; not a servant of the family was permitted to accompany us, lest they might lead to a discovery of my retirement.

We reached the end of our journey in two days, and met with a cordial reception from the lady of the house, whose name was Harris. 'Now, Emma' said Miss Hammond, 'you will be happy here; this is one of the best of women. You are to have the tuition of two little girls, and I hope you will fulfil your duty toward them.' My friend staid but one night with me, and when I found myself left with strangers, my heart almost died within me. Lady Hammond had so ordered it, that I was to pass for the daughter of a deceased friend of Mrs Harris's. Her house was a large gothic building, in a retired part of the country. My dear friend promised, at parting, to write to me, when it could be done with secrecy I loved her tenderly —and felt exquisite pain at our separation I thought incessantly on my situation, but most of all, on the ignorance of my birth, and implored heaven to give me some knowledge of my parents The image of him I so truly loved presented itself to my imagination, and vanity induced me to think that Edwin grieved for my departure I checked this vanity, as it arose, yet, to cease to think of him, I found impossible—though, conscious of the folly, I cherished the phantom in my breast

In a short time Mrs Harris engaged my esteem, she had an elegance of manners, and a sweetness of aspect, the power of which is easier felt than described. I found an unexpected consolation in a letter from Miss Hammond, much sooner than I had hoped—it was a cordial to my heart.

' May happiness await my ever dear Emma, in her new, but I hope, safe retreat The gentlemen of our family think my mother has consigned you to a lady who is going

to France I am distressed with anxiety for
Edwin —he looks ill and dejected, I wish I
could abate his care Lady Hammond desires
me to tell you, she never will withdraw her
friendship from you. Mrs Harris, as I before cautioned you. is ignorant of your real
story—never divulge it, but keep the name
of *Horton*, as first fixed on My *poor* family
are all well I went to them yesterday, the
woman asked particularly for you Mr
Digby has renewed his visits here, you
know he has long solicited my hand. He is
a worthy man, why should I. then, hesi-
tate? I shall acquaint you when I am in-
clined to change my situation Harriet is
now indulged in her wish, of having you out
of the house I have no happiness in her society, she chimes not with me in opinion
of any kind. She is ignorant of the place
of your retirement Lady Hammond sends
her kindest wishes, with your unalterable
friend's,

· C Hammond '

I was denied the comfort of writing an

answer to this dear friend, lest accident should lead to a discovery of my retreat

Mrs. Harris treated me like a parent Her son returned soon after my arrival He was a fine youth—his mother and sister idolised him Mrs Harris was blessed with four fine children she told me her only desire of life was to promote their welfare—that she chose this retired way of life as the best calculated to form their minds to virtue and innocence 'You, my dear girl, will assist me, in the arduous task, it is of more moment to me than adding thousands to what they already possess I am blessed with an ample fortue, yet have lost all that could make me truly happy' Tears filled her eyes 'Mr. Harris,' continued she, ' was one of the best of mankind When I married him, it was not without some reluctance, though I felt no other attachment, I thought it a serious matter to become a wife, and entered into the conjugal state with a thousand fears that women in general never suffer I am, however, certain I was happier afterwards than those who love more romantically. I found

I had reason to bless the hour that gave me a husband it is in every man's power to make a woman happy in wedlock. How many years did we live in a state of happiness! But, alas! he left me, never to behold him more he left me to mourn his loss for ever! A brother of his, who was immensely rich, wrote to him from the West Indies, that he had no children, and wished for Mr. Harris to settle his affairs, and return with him to Europe On the eve of his departure, I almost consented to go with him Oh! that I had perished in his arms! He hushed my fears and soothed my griefs, with the hope of a speedy return. Alas! the parting gales wafted my loved Edward from his doating Eliza. A storm arose, and the whole crew perished I never could have survived my husband's loss, had not solicitude for my children roused me from sorrow.'

I saw Mrs Harris was affected, and strove to amuse her, by turning the conversation, blessing heaven, that had provided me with such an amiable and feeling friend, who must know how to treat distress with humanity—

I had become the victim of sorrow, and my
health was much impaired by habitual melancholy, I was an object, such as a heart like
Mrs. Harris would delight to relieve, by those
thousand nameless and endearing attentions
that operate on a wounded spirit—Not more
refreshing are the early dews of heaven to the
withering plant, or the sweet descending
shower to the bosom of nature, than was the
cordial consolation of this kind and affectionate friend to my aching heart. The
ignorance of my birth, with a constant and
ever-longing desire to know from whom I de-
rived my being, kept my agitated frame in a
most uneasy state and the being torn from
him, who was father, brother, friend,—oh !
Edwin, you were all the tender tie to life I
ever knew,—you and your sister—cruel to
part me from them The following letter
will evince the unabated affection of my absent friends

‘ DEAR EMMA,

‘ As private opportunities so seldom offer,
I embrace this, to convince you, that you are

not forgot in the good wishes of your Charlotte I am miserable on Edwin's account;
his health is declining, and his spirits totally
depressed My mother is on the rack, to find
out the cause of his dejection. but in vain
The lady, I before mentioned to you, is now
here. we wish he may marry her—I am certain she returns his affection Her family
and fortune are desirable. Miss H is
very elegant, and perfectly accomplished.
My mother intends letting Edwin know
her wishes relative to the match It is hard
to judge whether it be love, or his natural
attention to the sex, that actuates him in his
conduct towards this lady, time only can
determine. We have prevailed on her to
stay a month longer it is pleasing to me to
have such a companion. since I have been
deprived of you Yesterday we had a plea-
sant ramble in the wood. we came to the
very spot where you were found, and I
thought of the moment when your infant
arms were stretched out. claiming our protection —' Here is the tree, Edwin,' said
I, ' that shaded poor little Emma.' but he

seemed not to heed me Miss H rambled away, as we were walking round the spot; and when we went in search of her, we found her in one of the arbours Edwin entered suddenly, and I saw her start and blush — What are those tender emotions, *I* never felt them for any man. You have often rallied me about Digby , but I am not in love with him. You have wished me in love, Emma, with the hope of seeing me married could I find such a man as Edwin, I don't doubt but Cupid would triumph , but, my dear girl, where could I find him ?—so amiable in mind and charming in person. Poor Miss H I feel for her—but if he returns her affection, all is as we wish.

‘ Lord George is making preparations for an excursion, he says, to France, and from thence to Germany · he has long intended it—he cannot bear to settle long in one place, so restless is his spirit

‘ We are all to dine from home to-day. Miss H. is dressing for the purpose , her gown is a white lustring, with lilac ribbon . a white chip hat, ornamented with flowers ,

she is really an elegant figure Edwin looks
better to-day than usual I see him on the
terrace, he little thinks that I am writing to
you I fear it will be long ere I can send you
another letter, yet, as Lord George is going
away, there will be the less danger of a discovery. Farewell, dear Emma.

' Yours sincerely,

' C. HAMMOND.'

Let those who have a heart judge of my
feelings, on perusing the letter of my friend,
and yet what hope could I flatter myself
with? He never can be mine, thought I—
may he be happy.

I daily strove, in vain, to conquer this
fond and foolish attachment I prayed earnestly to heaven, to strengthen me, I applied me attentively to the tuition of my
pupils, and strove to divert my thoughts
from the object that too powerfully engrossed
them I found, by experience, that religion
alone is the true consolation in all the calami-
ties which are incident to human nature.
I fled to it for succour, and found comfort

Edwin had early impressed the idea on my tender mind My friend's little poem drew from me a wish to divert my feelings at the time, and I wrote the following *Farewell to Hope*

Adieu! ye dreams of flattering, fond delight,
　Ye airy visions of my promis d joy,
Hope, kind deceiver, 's banish'd from my sight,
　Fond Hope, too often felt but to destroy

No more thy phantom haunts my troubled mind
　With the fond image of the youth I love,
His dear idea constant still I find,
　Does all my soul with generous wishes move

His heart affection, virtue, truth possess d,
　His sober judgment liveliest wit refined,
With gentlest manners, fancy, science bless d,
　He knew to form and captivate the mind

Were I possess'd of all this earth could give,
　Or power to call down blessings from above,
With lib ral hand, I'd give, would he receive,
　And share his joys, and soothe his cares with love

I found my heart relieved, by thus pouring fourth its complaints in these simple lines.

Mrs. Harris had but few visitors, she said,

she did not approve of the visitors of a day, but chose those, whom she knew were sincere friends. A companion and fellow-student of her son's came to spend a vacation with him, his name was Fortescue. He soon became enamoured with me, and made no secret of his attachment. He begged Mrs. Harris to intercede for him she advised me to listen to his suit; and asked me what objection I had. 'None at all, Madam,' said I, 'but a wish to live single a little longer.'— The fact was, I could not bear the idea of loving any man but Edwin. Young Harris and Fortescue were steadfast friends: it was grateful to the heart to behold such affection—so disinterested, with all the advantages of personal and improved endowments. The time of their departure was at hand Fortescue begged my answer, to cheer him on his journey. I told him I could not marry—thanked him for his prepossession in my favour, and that I should always esteem him. ' Esteem, my lovely girl, is too cold a word ; it was your heart I sought, but, since you deny me, I must, for evei, regret the loss of so inestimable a companion'

This amiable young man's passion was an addition to my sorrow , I had no vanity, or it would rathei have gratified me. A vain woman would have been flattered by the admiration of such a man as Fortescue, for he was captivating , but I could not return his affection, were he to place me on a throne. Oh, Edwin' had I never known thee, Foitescue and I might have been happy , but he was too good to be deceived I felt I must bring him a heart too cold foi an affection like his I closely examined my heart, and found that time only could suffer me, with honour, to engage in a union with another Our parting was very affecting, and seemed more like that of a fond brother and sister, than two strangers, almost uttei ly unknown.

The next vacation, Harris returned without his friend , he was called home to his mothei, who iesided in France. Harris gave us a detail of the parents of his friend, by the following letters, which he had foi-gotten to take with him, and which had been given by him to Harris, in whose possession they remained.

Mrs Fortescue to her Son.

' As none but a fond mother can have an idea of my solicitude, in being so long separated from a son, each day brings new anxieties. My nights are spent in sleepless watchings, and prayers for your preservation. As our separation will now be shortened, in consequence of the death of your cruel father, I will still continue my advice for your conduct, while you remain at college. I feared for that warmth of disposition, so apt to mislead young minds there was not a vicious seed in thy heart that I did not carefully eradicate, and now hope to see the blossoms of virtue spring in full perfection. When I married your father, I was thought to have attractions sufficient to secure the heart of any man, not wholly engrossed by sensual appetites, and yet he afterwards deserted me for a woman void of all sense and shame.

'During the first two years of our marriage, we lived in perfect harmony, but he invited a distant female relation, to spend part of the summer with us, who was vicious, vain, and artful, she seduced the affections of my husband, and he left me when you were but two years old. The shame of being thus forsaken, obliged me to live as retired as possible, to avoid censure. I educated you out of the allowance your father gave me, and when you were fit for college, he increased my annuity. I chose England for your residence, that you might not know your father. Had I been spared a daughter, which I had by him the year after your birth, I should have been happy. But I will be a mother to the houseless child of want. Your estate, which your father has encumbered, is yet sufficient, with my jointure, to do some good to others, let us make the right use of it, my son, and may you chuse a consort capable of sharing the sweets of virtue. When I see this accomplished, I shall, with hope, drop into my grave. Let no bad example shake your perseverance in virtue, for the slightest deviation from rectitude will be succeeded by remorse.

'The friend, you so often mention by the name of Harris, I hope will prove equal to your expectations—I know you are warm and steady in your attachments, one true friend is as necessary to your happiness as your existence, confide but in one, and may she be your friend in more than name!—Alas! I was deceived by him whom nature and duty ought to have made my protector. Your father seldom gave me his company, and, when he did, it was such as made his absence a blessing—Morose, gloomy, and ill-natured ——His guilty partner, on being detected, insulted me in his presence, and left our house with evident marks of her baseness He removed her to a private lodging, where she soon lay in of a son, from thence he took her to Brussels The four last years of his life I never beheld him. had I been apprised of his approaching dissolution, I should have visited him, with the hope that my presence would have melted

him to repentance. But the unhappy woman suffered him to die as he lived.

'The wretch, who robbed me of your father, and took him from my fond arms, had
the effrontery to write me a letter, soon after
his death, "hoping I would forgive her,
though she was conscious she had cruelly
injured me." She added, "that the influence of temptation had totally absorbed
her in guilt, but, now the cause was removed, she would endeavour to make me
some restitution, if I would favour her with
an interview." This I found impossible to
grant—my prudence could not admit of an
interview with so dangerous an enemy. I
declined her offer, and shortly after heard
that she had quitted France.

' I shall count the moments tedious till you
return, my son, and hope to be repaid, by
your filial affection, for all the miseries your
cruel father has occasioned me. My life,
since I met him, has been a continued scene
of woe. Will you, my boy, wipe away the
tears from the eyes of your afflicted mother?
Often have you curiously examined me,

concerning the cause of my repeated sorrow, but I continued silent on the subject,
while he lived, who was the cause of it.

'Farewell, my dear child—my continual
prayers are offered up for your preservation.
You will shortly be recalled by

'Your affectionate mother,

'Eliza Fortescue.'

[Meanwhile I received the following letters, descriptive of the transactions at Hammond Castle.]

Miss Hammond to her Friend.

'My dear Emma,

'Our family continues without any
change, except the departure of Lord
George. Edwin looks better, yet often
seems sad How I pity a heart like his,
alive to every virtuous sentiment'—May his
peace of mind be restored ' We never mention you, and it distresses me when any circumstance occurs, that reminds me of you.
My sister, I am convinced, has an envious
hatred towards you it is well you are placed

c 5

at such a distance from her, while I each day regret thy loss   One secret only have I concealed from thee—heai me on the subject now, and pardon my former want of confidence. All my affected apathy was only a covering to a heart much engaged.

‘ Henry Courtney is the friend of Edwin , I saw and loved him.   When first I beheld that engaging man, I was too young to form a liking but he came again, and, what to him was but idle gallantry, won an inexperienced heart, formed for tenderness.   It was my brother’s evident regard for him that first made me treat him with familiarity, which, by our being often together, ripened into a more tender attachment on my side— on his, only friendship tor I find he is shortly to be married   Never were my hours so delightfully spent as while he remained at Hammond Castle.   Edwin and he were inseparable, and his disposit.on and mine were so congenial, that we naturally loved the same objects.   Peil aps you may remember him , but you were too much detached from the family, and saw but few visitors.

'You know how much I stand in awe of my mother and sister, I could not make them the confidants of my situation, you alone I confide in It is a relief to my heart to disclose this secret to thee, my faithful Emma.

'But were not the necessary attentions, due to our sex, enough for Henry to bestow? Why did he hint more tender sentiments, but to gain my heart, and then to triumph in the victory? Oh! Henry, too well you knew of the conquest! And, will you believe it, Emma, he totally changed his conduct on the discovery; he grew reserved, and dropped all those attentions which won me. It is true, the theft of a woman's affections is not quite so atrocious as that of her honour, and yet it is a base action, unworthy of the manly mind I saw, a few days ago, a letter directed by Edwin to Henry Courtney, I felt an eager wish to know the contents, but honour forbade my violation of the secrets of these affectionate friends.

I often wish, Emma, (and, perhaps, I shall yet be gratified in it) that you and I

could live together, during the remainder of
our lives. Edwin is invited to attend the
nuptials of his friend, next month—Would
they were over! then I might be at rest.—
Pardon me, my friend, for so long concealing
what was so near my heart. Farewell.

'C. Hammond.'

Miss Hammond to her Friend.

' I am come to the knowledge of a secret,
but too late for my peace.—this amiable
Henry has been long engaged, and is now
going to fulfil it Edwin looks gay at the
approaching happiness of his friend. The
wedding is to be on Monday next; the lady
has no parents living. Her father was attached to the family of Courtney, and, when
dying, bequeathed her, and a large estate,
to Henry She lost her mother when an
infant. Her father idolized her, and her early
days were spent in retirement, which became
irksome to her as she grew up. Edwin
thinks her giddy and volatile—you know he
has uncommon penetration. To-morrow he
sets out for London. I shall send you a

full detail of the wedding. Edwin will write to me. Farewell, till I hear from him.

* * * * * *

'I again resume the pen, to tell you, the warmest congratulations attended the meeting of these affectionate friends. Edwin says Henry looks thoughtful—A certain proof of his good sense—it shows he has a proper idea of the state he is entering into. Every thing is prepared for the occasion· the lady's dress is costly to extravagance—Henry's plain and genteel. Alas! Henry is, ere this, the husband of another! But I will dwell no longer on a subject that ought to be for ever buried in oblivion by

'Your CH. HAMMOND.'

From the same to the same.

'Dear Emma,

'My brother is returned, and, I suppose, left his friend happy. He does not like the bride I am sorry for it—I would have Henry happy. Think what a time for Digby to renew his addresses to me! I may say, 'Was ever woman in such humour wooed?'

No· I could not encourage him, and so great is his wish of a connection with the family, that he has turned his attention to my sister, who receives his addresses, and a match will certainly take place when Harriet goes away. Would that I could recal you, now that Lord George is absent. That odious Ormsby, whom he made his companion, will be his ruin' I have often remonstrated on his profligate conduct. Lord George desired Ormsby to meet him, on his way to London—I wish they were never to meet. Ormsby knows how to indulge Lord George in his dissipation, while his purse is ever open to the necessities of others.

'Lady Hammond will now be somewhat gratified by seeing her children married. Digby's fortune is sufficient to indulge the vanity of Harriet, and, after their marriage, we shall remove to London for some time. I am well pleased that matters have taken this turn—I hope Harriet won't tyrannize over her husband, yet, as it is her natural disposition, it must break forth I fear there will be some discord, and it is even more tolerable in music than in the conjugal state.

‘ I was so taken up with the subject of Henry’s wedding, I forgot to tell you how closely I enquired into Edwin’s seeming regard for Miss H. He evaded my questions, and did not seem to like being spoken to on the subject.

‘ I hope you keep up your spirits; some presentiment intimates to me that heaven has a blessing in store for my Emma, and who wishes it more ardently than her

‘ Affectionate

‘ CH. HAMMOND?’

I may now, without further interruption, proceed with my own narrative. I lived with Mrs. Harris as happy as my situation would allow. Her girls grew up lovely, and daily improved, under my tuition. The world has produced few brighter characters than Mrs Harris, I could wish for no greater comfort than I enjoyed with her, but, to come to the knowledge of my parents, and once more to behold Edwin—Sweet would have been these gratifications to Emma. The kind Mrs. Harris showed me every mark of affection, and her efforts to make my life comfortable, joined with the letters of my Charlotte, supported me in a peaceful, yet pensive, state of mind : it was a pleasing sort of melancholy, and seemed to increase daily, as if a secret foreboding of what was to happen had taken possession of my unsuspecting heart.

One morning Mrs. Harris perceived an unusual dejection in my spirits, and requested my company, to spend the day with a family in the neighbourhood, where I would be roused from my langour; but I found I could not bring myself even to dress for the occasion ; and begged she would leave me behind. After continuing within all day, I thought the air would revive my spirits, and, in the evening, walked towards the end of the avenue . I saw a gentleman cross the adjacent meadow, but this did not alarm me. as it was a pathway. He shortly after came up to me, and, talking remarkably loud, ac-

costed me by my name, a carriage drove into
the field, from the adjacent road, and the unknown, holding both my hands, begged leave
to detain me a few minutes, during which
time the carriage came up, and I was lifted
into it, in a state of terror. 'Oh! whither,'
cried I, 'are you hurrying me, or what do
you intend?' The rapidity of our progress
was inconceivable the horses flew. I looked at the man on my right hand, and perceived his face covered with a black crape;
this occasioned fresh terror, especially as he
continued silent. Towards night they stopped at an inn, and changed horses, without
alighting, while this was doing, I thought
it was probable I had got into the hands of
Lord George, and, calling him by his name,
upbraided him with his barbarous conduct.
'So, you know me, then, my charming Emma?' cried he: 'I hoped you would not till
we had reached London.' 'Yes; I know no
other man could be so base as to use me
thus. Why did you deprive me of my happy and safe asylum?' 'I will take you to
my fond arms; you shall be mistress of all

I possess.' 'Thou monster!' returned I,
' death will rescue me from you.' I felt its
approach, and clasped my hands together in
an agony of despair There were provisions
in the carriage, and he requested me to take
some refreshment , but I refused. I felt
very ill , and, when we reached London,
was unable to stand or speak, with weakness
and terror. An ill-looking old woman and
a pert young girl were busy about me. I
requested to be left alone, but that was denied. A fever ensued, and next day I was
delirious, happy respite from misery! The
fever continued for fifteen days. My cruel
persecutor came so often to see me, that,
when I was able to sit up, he was seized
with my infection. Thus did Providence
interfere to save me from ruin.

When I was able to walk about, I begged
pen, ink, and paper from the old woman , but
she looked at me with a sneer of contempt.
' My master has ordered you every attention
his house can afford, but that,' said she. —
I could not bribe her, for I was penny-
less. There was not a ray of hope left for

an escape from my enemy, but his death!
and that was hourly expected yet, if it happened, I had another to combat, still more
odious, in his friend, the villanous Ormsby!
for it was he who assisted in this plan of car-
rying me off, nay, he took advantage of his
lordship's illness, and made his addresses.
He told me the plan was to take me to France,
whither they were going; and that, if I
would make him happy, by marrying him,
he should find means of delivering me from
Lord George. I did not totally deprive him
of hope, in consequence of which, the false
wretch told me all he knew respecting the intention of his employer. I expected each
day would rid me of one of these monsters,
by death; but was mistaken, for the fever
abated, and he recovered in a fortnight, at
the expiration of which, he came to visit me.
He complimented me on my looking so well,
which I could not return, for he was like a
spectre. ' Well, my charming Emma,' said
he, ' I hope all obstacles to our union will
shortly be removed my sickness has caused
a long delay. Look on me, in future, as a

man capable of protecting you, and whose greatest wish is, to see you happy.' ' Then restore me to my late protector , you have no right to rob me of my liberty. I never will consent to your infamous proposals ; and I think you had better spend your time in thanks to heaven, that has not cut you off in the midst of your sins ' ' None of your cant-ing,' cried he, ' I shall be able to pursue my journey in a week, and must get a travelling dress prepared.' ' And I can tell you,' an-swered I, ' your travelling dress will be your coffin '' At these words he grew as pale as death, and got up, but tottered so, I could see a relapse would ensue. He muttered something as he left the room, and seemed highly offended · perhaps, had he been able to stay out of bed, I should have felt the effect of his malice ; but a more tedious sick-ness than the former seized him, during which Ormsby told me how they got intelli-gence where I was placed. The letters Miss Hammond conveyed to me were what led to a discovery.

One day, finding the door of my apartment open, I ran into the street, without knowing where to go I thought all who followed me were coming to take me, and every countenance I met, seemed as if they were too busily employed to pity me. I walked till I was almost exhausted, and at length ventured into the shop of a bookseller I called a woman aside, and told her my distress, hoping she would assist me. ' If you are in distress, young woman,' said she, ' go out again.' I tried several more, but got an answer to the same purpose Merciful God!' said I, ' must I perish for want in the streets? where shall I find a shelter, or place to lay my wretched head?' I again entered the shop of a milliner, in whose countenance I traced affability and sweetness, I threw myself on my knees, and begged protection for one night, and told her part of my unhappy story. ' Hard would that heart be,' said she, ' that would refuse thee shelter, and woe to that man who has thus oppressed thee.' ' May heaven requite thee, for thy compassion to a stranger,' replied I , 'and may the comfort thou hast be-

stowed on me, be tenfold rewarded in heaven, where mercy to the stranger is promised to be repaid.' 'Were all the creation as
sordid as a certain part of it, the needy
would perish; but there are hearts to be
found, which, though liable to imposition,
will follow the first dictate of compassion to
a fellow-creature in distress, and risk the
hazard of imposture. Every child of want
ought to find pity from those who have it in
their power to bestow relief let their misfortunes be even of their own creating, still
we are bound to relieve them. This is universal benevolence—this is the law of him,
who is mercy itself.'

These were the words of this angelic woman She got me some refreshments, and a
comfortable bed, where I rested my sorrowful
head, and slept sound I got up, thankful to
heaven for its goodness to me, and wrote a
long letter to my friend Mrs. Harris, telling
her all that had befallen me, which letter I
afterwards found she never received. Mrs.
Towers was induced to give me employment, on finding I could work expertly with

my needle. The first thing I took in hand was
a mourning suit for a widow ; the next was a
wedding one for a lady of the same description, who had buried her fourth husband,
and was going to marry the fifth! I laughed at the idea. ' I suppose,' said Mrs.
Towers, ' if you lost one husband, you would
never supply his place with another ? I hope,
in my heart, you will get one to your mind.'
I sighed, and called for some materials for
the work Mrs. Towers offered me money to
buy clothes, and I took her maid along with
me. We had not passed through many
streets, when surprise almost deprived me of
the power of motion, I thought I saw the
shadow of Fortescue, but it was not the
shadow, it was the real substance. After
he had passed, recollecting me, he turned,
and caught me by the hand ' Emma!
dearest of women, is it you I am blessed
once more in beholding?' He ordered a
sedan instantly, and came along with me,
where I directed, I brought him to Mrs
Towers, and introduced him as a friend.
She received him politely, and I requested

her to inform Mr Fortescue how I came to her, and the treatment of Lord George.

Fortescue was unable to hear it out, he rose from his seat, his passion grew to its height, calling out, ' Villain! monster! he shall meet the reward of his crimes!—this arm shall give the blow, and rid the earth of a wretch, a disgrace to human nature. I shall find him out, and revenge thy wrongs, thou innocent victim' He attempted to rush out of the room, but we held him, and shut the door ' Oh! be calm, Sir,' cried I, ' in pity to my feelings, compose yourself let no worse consequence ensue, I am now freed from his tyranny, and leave him to the all-wise disposer of good and evil It is true I should have perished in the streets, but for the humanity of Mrs Towers may heaven reward her.' ' She shall be amply rewarded,' replied the generous youth. ' I expect none,' said she, ' but the pleasure I have already experienced in the action there was an air of truth in the story and appearance of Miss Emma ' ' Yes,' replied Fortescue, ' she is truth itself, and if you, Mrs. Towers, will accompany her, I will take her, this moment, to the protection of my mother, who is lately come to reside in this city ' I thanked him for his kindness, and told him I should feel my dependence less, by remaining with Mrs. Towers, as I could assist her in her business , that I expected answers to letters I had written to Mrs Harris, who would again receive me, when she heard of all that befel me   Mrs. Towers left the room, and Fortescue said, ' I well know, Emma' that you fear a renewal of my addresses , and delicacy will not let you take the shelter of my mother's house but here I vow, never to trouble you more with my passion, unless you find you can return it. Your happiness is now my sole object. I could have pressed for a return of my affection, but I saw your reluctance   Still friendship actuates me, and I feel the warmest wishes to serve you , yes, I would do it at the hazard of my life , and could not wish for a greater gratification, than taking a proper revenge on him who has so cruelly injured you.'   rget it, Sir,' said I, ' it cannot now, in any degree, be useful to me that you should subject yourself to danger—but the contrary.' 'Then come with me to the best of women, let not my once declaring for you a tender passion, prevent you from enjoying, with us, the sweets of ease and affluence' I could not consent to this kind offer, and saw him depart, silent and melancholy.'

Mrs. Towers was much charmed with Fortescue, yet seemed pleased I was to remain longer with her. The following day brought me a letter from Fortescue, inclosing a bank note of fifty pounds. Mrs. Fortescue also wrote, in her son's letter, assuring me I might have accepted the offer of her house, which should ever be open to the unfortunate. She said I was no stranger to her, as she had often heard her son mention every individual of Mrs. Harris's family, and she promised herself much pleasure in waiting on me in a few days.

She came accordingly, accompanied by a beautiful young lady a splendid retinue attended them, and, in my life, I thought I had never beheld so lovely a woman as Mrs.

Fortescue She accosted me familiarly, and told me she came to take me home with her, but that, whenever I pleased, I might return to Mrs. Towers

I took a tender leave of that charitable benefactress, and she parted from me with reluctance, Mrs Fortescue making her a promise, that she would send me to visit her as often as I wished

Peace again began to dawn on my almost desponding soul Mrs Fortescue treated me with the respect and affection of a person of consequence · her son's behaviour was like that of a fond brother, and the lovely Harriet's society was to me most pleasing, I thought she was calculated to make young Fortescue happy. Thus was the poor and unfriended Emma surrounded with affluence, and, what to her was more desirable, with hearts congenial to her own

I wrote again to Mrs. Harris and Miss Hammond, and had the additional happiness of getting an answer from Mrs. Harris, informing me, that she felt the bitterest pangs for the manner in which she had lost me, hav-

ing never heard the smallest hint of what was
my fate, that her daughters pined in my absence, and concluded with an earnest desire
of my return She congratulated me on the
miraculous escape I had from so dangerous
an enemy to female chastity, Lord George
informed me her son was gone to travel, and
that she expected, on his return, to find him
much improved, that Lady Hammond talked
of coming to live in town, in hopes it might
be an inducement to Mr. Hammond to marry   I concealed nothing of my life from
Mrs Fortescue, but my being left in the
wood, and that particular Mrs Harris was
unacquainted with, at the desire of Lady
Hammond

Few days passed in which I was not witness to some new act of philantropy in Mrs
Fortescue. Her son indulged her with his
own purse, and both hers and that excellent young man's were continually open to
the indigent.

I had now passed half a year with Mrs.
Fortescue, and begged her permission to return to Mrs. Harris, who importuned me for

my company I was preparing to go, and had part of my clothes packed up, the generous Mrs Fortescue loaded me with presents, and indulged me in a visit to Mrs. Towers, who prayed heartily for my success, and I, by the bounty of my benefactress, had it in my power to bestow some little presents on her girls, as tokens of my gratitude. A day was fixed on for my departure, but so ill could we bear a separation, that another and another succeeded. Young Fortescue was to accompany me, though his friend was absent. His mother wished for an acquaintance with Mrs Harris, and hoped, when she came to town, for that pleasure. ' We shall often hear from you, Emma. Believe me, it is with reluctance I part with you, but I would not be the means of detaining you any longer from your old friend

On the day mentioned for my departure, Mrs Fortescue received a letter—the contents of which she did not let us know, but told me, my journey must be deferred, as the carriage, that was to bring me, must go with her. She returned in the evening, and taking me to walk in the garden, enquired minutely concerning my birth, that she had got a hint of my being left in the wood of Hammond Castle I confessed it was true, and my agitated heart beat violently to know who made this discovery. Oh! thought I, perhaps, I shall yet be restored to my parents

Mrs Fortescue would not inform me of any of the particulars, but said, I could not go away for a day or two The following day she went again, and I waited her return in the utmost suspense but, oh! gentle reader, what were my emotions, when she folded me in her arms, exclaiming, 'Oh! my child! my long lost darling!' She held me a considerable time in her fond embrace, I felt as if my heart bounded from its place, and never would be at rest again. Delightful emotion!—a mother! Her son remained in silent astonishment, then taking my hand, 'And are you then my sister, Emma?'— Gracious God! from whence arose this discovery?' 'I will satisfy you, my children," said my mother; ' and for ever blessed be that Providence who has restored me to my daughter. My children, you were all the comfort I had left, for the loss of your unnatural father, and Emma was snatched from my paternal arms by the same wretch who was the cause of all my sorrows when death approached, she sent for me, to relieve her troubled conscience, and made her last confession, which was nearly in the following words —

'Mr Fortescue had promised to marry her, at my decease, and she owned she had often premeditated to poison me She knew Mr. Fortescue was extremely fond of his little daughter, and, lest the child should withdraw his affections from herself, employed a woman, of the name of Elvin, to watch my house, and, one day, as little Emma was playing in the lawn, the wretch carried her away to her employer, who gave her twenty guineas to put my babe to death! But the poor woman, on getting the gold, removed from Brussels, where she had been reduced to extreme want, and took my Emma, with an intention to share with her what

Providence pleased to send · but, on receiv-
ing intelligence of the death of some friends
in England, from whom she had expected
relief, she could no longer support her helpless charge, and begging was now become
her only refuge, as her husband became sick-
ly. As she travelled through the country,
she was told of a young lady that lived at
Hammond Castle, who was very charitable,
and, taking a lodging in a village near it,
dressed Emma, one day, as neatly as she
could, and pursuing a gravel walk, that led
through the improvements, while she lulled
my child asleep in her arms, she laid her
down, under the shade of a large tree, by a
walk which was frequented by the family, and
going in an hour after she left her, found the
babe had been taken away, the wretch added,
that this Mrs. Elvin had written to her some
years ago, and informed her, that she was often fed by the hand of the child she was
hired to murder, and told her where she had
placed her, that she and her family would
have perished, but for the bounty of Miss
Hammond, that Emma was a fine girl, and

she exulted in the happy residence she had placed her in , that her motive for giving her this intelligence, was, with the hope that she would restore Emma to her relatives.'

My mother then opened a little bundle, which contained the clothes I had on the day I was stolen away, the richness of which made my betrayer covet them for her own child , but, it being a son, she laid them by, and now restored them to my mother, as a proof of my being her daughter. ' I left this wretched woman,' continued my mother, ' in the agonies of death She told me she came on purpose after me to London, when she grew ill, that I might be reconciled to her, and with the hope, that restoring to me my daughter would, in some measure, atone to heaven for the injuries she had done me.'

Thus did happiness diffuse its sunny beams over my soul, which each succeeding day ripened to the fullest perfection. My beloved mother went again, like a forgiving angel, to see the dying sinner, who lay tortured with remorse. Guilt! O destroying guilt!

bitter is thy cup to the mind of those, who
arrive at that awful period, when all the anxious and agitating cares of this chequered
life dwindle into nothing · then it is, that a
life spent without a crime cheers the dying
creature with hope!

My mother exerted herself to console the
penitent, who expired in the utmost agony
of body and mind, but we leave her to the
just dispensation of him who promised pardon to the penitent; and bless him, who has
given us grace to avoid similar guilt.

Our days glided on in perfect enjoyment;
we saw but few visitors—any intrusion was
irksome to us—so totally were we engrossed
by the late happy discovery. I exulted in
the idea of introducing a mother and brother
to Lady Hammond and her family, whom
the proudest might be vain to claim an affinity with. My brother seemed to have no
wish beyond making his family happy, by his
affectionate attentions.

'Well,' thought I, 'good has arisen from
my attachment to Edwin,' and I sighed at
the recollection, but my brother knew not

the cause. I began to think that Harriet grew fond of him, and pitied her, knowing the consequence of a tender passion myself which I could safely say, was now almost buried in oblivion. I found other claims on my heart, and began to look on my attachment to Edwin as a dream, which once afforded some delight, but brought a cruel reverse, in a separation ; and, as I now felt tranquillity of mind, to which I had hitherto been a stranger, I strove to subdue feelings, that would otherwise have been fatal to my peace.

Mrs Harris was soon informed of my good fortune, and the only bar I had to perfect joy, was not having received any letter from Miss Hammond, to whom I had written several times. This neglect depressed my spirits, for who, that ever loved a friend as I did, could bear the loss of their affection ? In the sunshine of our days, friends will smile upon us, but Charlotte had proved herself a friend in my adversity, and I hoped that some mischance had happened her letters to me. I was soon put out of suspense, by the arrival of one from her well-

known hand, with the warmest congratulations. She told me, that Lady Hammond
and Edwin added then, and that Lord
George had written from Brussels, but did
not mention when he would return home.
She also informed me her family would
shortly be in town, and have the pleasure of
meeting my newly discovered relations.—
This news made my heart throb with rapture at the idea of once more beholding Edwin Yet I was apprehensive that my tranquillity would be disturbed by an interview
with a man who was once so dear.

I was summoned to wait on Lady Hammond, on her coming to town. Both her
ladyship and my beloved Charlotte received
me with joy. My agitation abated, on hearing Mr. Hammond was not at home, but
was expected to dinner. Every time the parlour door was opened, I started, ' I wish the
interview were over,' thought I, ' for our
imagination paints worse than the reality '

At length Mr Hammond was summoned
to dinner, affection revived on his appearance, and but for my strongest efforts, my

feelings must have betrayed me. I scarcely
ventured to look at him, and he said little
more than that he was sincerely glad to hear
of my finding so amiable a mother

When dinner was over, I retired with
Charlotte, to talk over the many strange occurrences, which had taken place since our
separation. She sent to my mother to let her
know she could not part with me for that
night, and that next day she and the family
would visit her

Edwin appeared again at tea—he seemed
pensive—Charlotte and I played and sung;
I played a few soft tunes. We begged one
from Edwin, on the flute, but he refused.—
'Well,' thought I, ' Edwin is not even glad
to see me, little did I imagine he would receive me so coldly.' His sister asked him,
whether he would accompany us to Mrs.
Fortescue's, to whom Emma was going to introduce them? He answered, he would, and
next morning, the carriage being announced,
we all went in great state. Lady Hammond
was so captivated with my mother, that a

constant intercourse, from that day, took place between the families.

My brother and Edwin became intimate companions . and with pleasure did I behold their growing attachment.

I received a letter from Mrs. Harris, in which she mentioned that she was coming to town, and longed to be witness to my happiness, which gave her sincere pleasure, as she loved me tenderly.

Lady Hammond proposed to our family an excursion to Hammond Castle, where we might enjoy all the delights of the approaching summer. She said Edwin could not be happy long in town, as he ever disliked it: so the jaunt was agreed on by all parties.

From my heart I exulted in the idea of once more beholding the enchanting shades of Hammond Castle, where nature and art were both combined to make the scene delightful. Charlotte and I were almost frantic with joy, what charming rambles shall we have'—our brothers too, will be with us, and friendship and harmony will go hand in hand.

Our stay was limited to two months, and we all set out, and travelled most agreeably.

On coming in sight of that ancient dwelling, I felt a thousand tender emotions. The old domestics received me with astonishment; a spaniel, grey with age, flew to me, and put his paws about my neck—Edwin was his master!

On the day after our arrival, we were to dine in a temple, in the most sequestered part of the wood, a river surrounded the little island which contained this beautiful retreat.

Charlotte and I were busily employed in preparations for the rural fête; and, as we rambled from the temple to the house, often stopped to admire the flowery banks of the stream, and listen to the murmur of the torrent descending on the rocks beneath the wild flowers blooming around, filled the fancy with delight.

We passed a day of social happiness, but the next was turned into gloom, on my part, by the arrival of Miss H. who came to welcome Lady Hammond on her return, which was much sooner than she expected. I did not hope for bliss greater than that I enjoyed, in the sweet society of those I loved ; but a rival, I did not like to behold, and I saw too, that Edwin received her with much greater affection than he did me, nay, if envy could have found a place in my breast, the attentions he paid her would have excited it.

Charlotte remarked that I became gloomy. ' What ails my girl? come, call the lads and lasses, and we will go amuse ourselves with a ramble , but, in that proposal, how was I mortified to see Edwin offer his arm to Miss H. and neglect me. ' I am now his equal,' thought I , ' but why should I expect his assiduity—he never sought my love—he loves Miss H.'

I sauntered away, unheeded, from the party, to meditate on my folly. I entered a grotto, where I sunk into a melancholy reverie, from which I was roused by the noise of the woodman's strokes. I proceeded in search of the company, but they had quitted the improvements, and returned home, where I

followed them hastily, and found them all at
tea—Edwin was seated close by Miss H. He
had the politeness to hand me my tea   I
was rallied a good deal for being so fond of
separating from the company. 'What would
you infer from it?' said my brother.   Miss
H. replied, ' That she is in love.'   I blushed ; and casting a look of contempt at her,
said, ' You judge of me by yourself, I suppose.' 'No,' replied she; 'for I did not stray
away, as you did, to complain to the silent
groves, of some absent swain '   I thought
her impertinent, and wished to retaliate, but
judged it best to be silent   though the pert
manner in which she rallied me, I could ill
bear, as I felt too powerfully the truth   But
a letter, in few a days, put an end to all my
tedious doubts and apprehensions , it was
delivered by my brother   I knew the hand,
and felt so embarrassed—I put it in my
pocket, and betook me again alone to the
woods, and, under that very tree, whose shel-
tering branches first received me, I read an
avowal of Edwin's affection, as follows:—

' Dear Emma,

' I address you not in the style of a romantic lover, but in the endearing language
of the purest affection —Until I lost you, I
was a stranger to the passion that now fills
my heart.—In your infant days, I found
great delight in your innocent society , but,
as you grew up, my heart was subdued by
your opening charms ·—you are now surrounded with friends, a mother and brother,
who adore you, and if in your breast you
can find room for a yet more tender connection, accept the heart and hand of your

' Truly devoted

' EDWIN HAMMOND.'

Now were all jealous fears at an end,
I returned home, Miss H   recommenced
her raillery, and said she saw me from the
window going and coming alone · I could
now with patience let her proceed , for the
fact was, she felt an unreturned affection for
Edwin.   In a few days he took her away,
and the time we intended to stay at the castle
being nearly spent, we had thoughts of re-

turning to town, and my brother told me that
Edwin only waited the consent of his mother
and mine to our union, after he declared himself to me. Their consent being obtained, no
bar remained to prevent its taking place on
our arrival in town.

I had not seen Edwin since I received the
letter, and, at our first interview afterwards, I
felt confusion   he asked me to take a walk
with him, and I accordingly complied.

He renewed his wishes in the warmest
and most gentle manner. I accused him of
coldness and ill-nature to me, on our first
meeting · ' Ah ! my dearest Emma,' replied he, " that apparent coldness was excessive tenderness. On the day you arrived at our house in London, a giddiness
seized me, the moment my servant told me
you were in the parlour. I could not immediately come to you, and, I own, I
wished to discover some involuntary token
of your tenderness before I declared myself.
These were my motives for reserve. It was
painful to me; but now, during the remainder of my existence, my attentions, my

unalterable affections, shall be ever devoted to my long-loved Emma! My love grew with your increasing charms. As an aged oak seems formed, by its nature, for shelter-ing the tenderest companions of the forest, so would I shelter you, at a time you most required protection, but now you are per-fectly independent, and if I am so happy as to call you mine, I shall be sensible of the blessing you confer.'

On my return I saw joy in the faces of all my friends· Charlotte embraced me, and called me sister, saying, ' there needed not that tie to unite us in affection —it is a long attachment on the part of my brother.'

A day was fixed for our return to town, and Charlotte, Edwin, and I, travelled in the same carriage. Lady Hammond, Mr. Fortescue, and my brother in another;— the most tender conduct on the part of Ed-win made the journey doubly pleasing, and an early day was fixed for our union.

My generous brother was lavish in his presents on the occasion, but, in the midst of all this apparent felicity, I began to

fear that it was not a reality , and in the af-
tionate attentions of my loved Edwin, my
heart felt a kind of sorrow, contrary to what
one in my situation might indulge   Edwin
accused me of a coldness foreign to my
heart.—I alone was sad,—something in the
likeness of Lord George whispered to my
imagination, " Edwin never shall be yours "

Lady Hammond proposed to me to take
an airing, as I seemed low-spirited. We
went, attended only by one servant, as we
intended going but a few miles. The gentleman promised to follow us , but, before
they could come up, our coach was stopped by a number of armed men, while one
held the postillion, the carriage door was
opened, and I was dragged out and placed in
another, whilst the firing of pistols, and the
rapidity of the motion of the carriage, overpowered my senses. On my recovery, I
looked wildly around, and saw by my side
the source of all my woe '

' You see, my charmer, I have got you
again,' cried he   ' I have spies on all your
actions, and that at a time you are little

aware. So, you were to become the wife of Edwin !—O ! it was he that made you re- ject me ?"

After some hours travelling, I was taken in- to an inn, near the road side· the inhuman monster then began to upbraid me, and told me he would not use me ill, if I would swear never to become the wife of Edwin,— he gave me my choice. I was dumb to all his proposals ; indeed I was unable to reply. He took from his pocket a book : ' There is no time to be lost,' said he, ' swear, or, by the contents of this, I will satisfy my long frustrated hopes.' Just as I held the book, the door, (though locked), was burst open, and, I beheld Edwin and my brother enter. A pistol lay charged on the table, and the contents were fired by the diabolical brother, at the breast of my loved Edwin The inn became a scene of confusion, and I remained in a state of stupefaction. During my bro- ther's efforts to support me and my wound- ed lover, the assassin escaped I held my hand close to the bleeding wound of my Ed- win, while my brother sent for a surgeon, who, when he had examined it, said he had good hopes, and, lifting him into the carriage, placed me by his side, with orders to go as easy as possible.

It is needless to say, the family at home were in the utmost consternation. Lady Hammond's grief was not to be described, but as hopes of her son's recovery were given by the surgeon, and all possible care taken, we continued for several days in the most excruciating anxiety. On the tenth day after he received the wound, he grew worse, and became delirious. I was seated by his bedside, and all his anxious friends about him. Emma,' said he, ' the hand of Heaven has thrown a bar between us!'' ' No, my life,'' said I, ' it is the hand of a villain.' ' Oh! no, my love,' replied the dying angel, ' it is Heaven that permits all the events of life—I will make you mine to-morrow · send for all my friends to attend my wedding,—to-morrow I will be——— '
He began to rave, and then fell into a lethargic state. ' Alas! you are going fast,' thought I, I could not bear to take my eyes

off him, while his other friends remained in
silent woe in the next room.—The doctor
gave him up for lost

Hope revived us a few days longer; he
seemèd collected, and ate more than usual ;
but, alas ! the wound was deep ! ' The
dart sunk into thy heart, oh ! Edwin, my
love, and has left a wound in mine, which,
through this vale of misery, can never be
healed , and must death now part us, by
the cruel hand of a brother, infatuated by
prejudice and passion ! Mistaken man ! how
hast thou heaped wrongs on the innocent,
and laid up for thyself never-ending remorse ! for that period will overtake thee,
come when it may, that the arrows you
have discharged against two fond hearts will,
most undoubtedly, recoil on thy own wretched conscience , and that dying angel, you
have sent before his time to eternity, will
sorely imbitter your moments, when you are
called to quit a world in which you lived as
if you were ever to be its inhabitant ! Oh !
Edwin ! Edwin ! you know how to live !
best of friends, and worthiest of mankind !

how shall I support thy loss? and thy fond mother and sister, who will supply the tender son and affectionate brother to them? But I will on my knees implore that Heaven, which I must have offended, or should not thus be afflicted, I will petition its mercy in pity for those mourners.'

As I was thus contemplating, and began to sink into a state of languor, my mother and Lady Hammond entered the room; both looked as if their hearts were breaking: ' Go, my love,' said these tenderest of friends, ' seek the alleviation of repose, and we will watch our precious charge till morning.'

I began to undress, when, thinking of my dear Charlotte, who was in the next room, I stepped to look at her, and perceived she was in a very uneasy sleep I knelt by her bed, and prayed, to compose my agitated spirits, when, in the first effort to beg for resignation, I was disturbed, and obliged to rise from my feeble knees, by Charlotte, who, rising up in the bed, exclaimed, ' Where am I? who has murdered my brother? Is he dead? I have heard that Edwin is gone! Oh! Emma, are you there?' 'Yes, my love, I am, how have you rested?' 'Oh! very ill; I had tormenting dreams, but I shall get up and visit my brother.' 'You had better lie still,' said I, 'and I will go enquire for you, there can be no change since I left him.' 'Oh!' said she, 'my head aches, but I will go—all my waking moments are too short to behold my Edwin!' I fell on her neck, and embraced her; we both vented our distressed hearts in tears and fruitless wailings. When we entered the room, our eyes were again blessed with a sight of our Edwin, sitting up in his bed, supported by his mother, who looked with delight on all around, a ray of hope, it seems, had darted its bright beams into her soul, and she, at that moment, thought, 'My son will live!' her eyes spoke it plainly. I cast a penetrating, anxious look at my love, which he returned with tenderness but, oh! how dim was that eye, which so oft beamed on me with delight. I felt that I was beloved by the most valuable of mankind, but my own

natural timidity would not allow me to cherish
the thought—yet he looked his whole soul.
I still suffered nothing but doubts—I had few
hopes to sustain me, till I read it from his own
pen, and it was afterwards confirmed by his
dear lips—and now must we be separated for
ever by death! can it be? Oh! just Providence!
must I behold the manly form of Edwin in-
animate as dust? Oh! I see, I see, my love
is going fast! I cannot survive him!" The
perturbation of my ideas brought on a faint-
ing fit. Edwin observed me first, he made
signs to my mother that I was changing colour—so observant was he of all my emotions.
I found my hand clasped in his, when I recovered. I thought he looked animation to
my exhausted spirits, I returned it with all
the tenderness I was capable of and, judge
you, who have ever felt the heart-rendings of
real sorrow, in what a state of hope and fear
I was suspended, when the surgeon pro-
nounced his pulse better!—A ray of dawn-
ing hope darted on the souls of all around
the bed we fell on our knees, to implore
that gracious Providence to spare our dar-

Iing Edwin symptoms of convalescence appeared every hour. Though this wound was
deep and dangerous, and the loss of blood
great, yet, from the natural soundness of a
constitution which had not been enfeebled
by dissipation or irregularities of any kind,
in less than a week from this period, he recovered fast. Judge ye, who ever felt the
mother's care or the sister's affection, what
must have been then feelings on this happy
change I shall not attempt to paint my own
—let silence rest upon it

Edwin recovered so fast, that we committed him to the care of his servant at night,
and the whole family revived in health and
spirits. He was soon able to sit up in his
bed, and began to walk about the room, and
recover strength, yet his spirits were visibly
oppressed. He ordered his man to have his
horse ready to take an airing, but the doctor
requested he would not, for a week longer—
as then he would be perfectly out of danger.
The time being expired, he took an airing in
the carriage, and said he found new life in
exercise, after the long confinement He

continued it for another week, and, by
that time, was apparently restored to
health, yet a gloom hung over his open
manly countenance, and a tear was often
seen to steal from his eye —the natural
bloom of his fine complexion, which had
faded in consequence of loss of blood, often
changed to a death-like paleness. We all
remarked it to each other and feared much,
he had some hidden complaint, unknown to
his physician or himself.

A few days afterwards, he secretly left
Hammond Castle, attended by his servant
and a letter, directed to Lady Hammond, ex-
plained his motive for this seemingly un-
friendly conduct.

‘ My dearest mother!

‘ WITH a heart torn with anguish, I
could not take a personal farewell of my
dear friends but, as Providence has spared
my life, I think it my duty still to preserve
it (if I can) from him who is determined,
if I become the husband of Emma, to destroy us both. The faithful Thomas, who

alone is to be the companion of my exile, has been told by a confidant of Lord George, of a diabolical plot against me, worse than death itself, and the innocent object of my affection would also become a sacrifice to the vindictive malice of my unnatural brother Comfort her in my absence —Oh! that she had still remained ignorant of my affection for her, she might then have blessed some happier man, who may not be persecuted as I am with the most unrelenting cruelty If I can with secresy, I will let you hear from me when I arrive at my intended retreat, but if I remain silent, be assured, my loved friends, it will be for the preservation of my life. The very posts are now watched by spies, and creatures bribed for the purpose of knowing all my actions To account to you and my friends for my absence, I could not hurt your feelings, by painting the unparalleled vices of a brother whom I would not even now injure, and lest his life should end with ignominy, and I be sent before my time to another world, I have torn myself away from all I hold dear on earth — let not Emma grieve, I have the preservation of her honour and her life in view — Though we be not united here, we shall yet meet Be comforted, my dear mother, and may blessings attend you' whatever befal

    ' Your affectionate

      ' and dutiful son,

        EDWIN HAMMOND '

All comfort was again vanished on reading this, sorrow filled each heart, tears each eye ; though we should a short time before have borne a separation when death seemed hovering over his head . now that separation felt like death. But, alas! we had both to sustain, for, in less than a month after his departure, the newspaper brought the following dreadful intelligence —' Died, at Bath, after a few days illness, Edwin Hammond, Esq. of Hammond Castle '

My brother first read it his colour changed, and the newspaper dropped from his hand,—he stopped, after just pronouncing, Edwin. I caught the sound, and eagerly snatching up the fatal news, sunk lifeless on reading what followed, and for some days was insensible to the many fellow-mourners I had to share my sorrow

I lay in a state of stupefaction for a week, and, when I recovered my reason, found all around me in the deepest affliction. My affectionate brother, though he felt much for the loss of his friend, used all his tender efforts to calm my grief, but time alone could in any degree blunt the edge of my sorrow The afflicted mothers tried to comfort each other mine was endowed with that Christian fortitude, which the mother of Edwin was deficient in at the hour of trial, and fell short of that celestial ray of hope, which cheers the soul where religion is its support'——Their education had been dissimilar.——— Lady Hammond had been bred in the lap of luxury, and untaught in the useful lessons of early piety, which had been the only support of my mother in all the misfortunes that attended her un n with my father

Lady Hammond could not bear one day's

absence from my mother; grief preyed on her most poignantly, and my aching heart was tortured with grief, which no time or place could alleviate. Though we endeavoured to comfort each other, it seemed but a useless effort, until the arrival of a friend, the most effectual of all medicine to an afflicted mind.

That friend was young Harris, a pleasing guest, just arrived from his travels, of which he gave a most entertaining account The joy my dear brother felt, after so long a separation, was unparalleled, both possessed hearts capable of the warmest sentiments of friendship he had now got a companion in his task of comforting, who used all his vivacity to keep up our spirits he gave us a humorous narrative of his travels. He was much improved both in person and manners, a little time began to wear away the keenness of our sorrow, we confined ourselves solely to our own own family, and hoped each day for the arrival of some tidings from the faithful Thomas, but Thomas came not. he had one brother, the only near relation living, who went in search of him to Bath, but got no intelligence whatever, though he found out the house that he had lodged in. All the information he could obtain was, that Thomas had quitted Bath immediately after the death of his master.

The two friends left no effort in their power untried to amuse us. ' You and Harris,' said my brother, ' have always been friends ' ' Yes, Fortescue,' replied he, ' you were the only inmate my heart ever could acknowledge, even in my late travels I have been disgusted with my own sex, and their practices, and those of the other were in general only calculated to ex- cite similar contempt You know that I ever admired and loved the softer sex, and therefore avoided the company of those who might lessen them in my esteem. Sweet is the society of women, such as I am conver- sant with, and happy were the hours I spent in my own family, when surrounded with females. I was proud, on my return home, to find my sisters so much improved, but who might not profit by the example of your sister !"—' Mr Harris,' said I, ' you have learned the language of compliment, though you want to insinuate that you are free from the arts of your sex !"——' Well,' continued he, ' do not be too severe, and I will tell you a short story, simple but interesting

' I should have profited more by my travels but for the stupidity of my tutor I wished for one to communicate my remarks to, as animated as myself " Give me a companion," says Yorick, " on my way, were it only to remark to him how our shadows lengthen as the sun goes down ," and my dull companion was only fit to look at such things as shadows. Now, ladies, the manners of all the foreign courts, which I have visited, and all the beauties of nature and art, though they excited my admiration, never touched my feelings like the misfortunes of poor Letty, which happened, I may say, at home.

' My Tutor had a daughter in Wales, whom he wished to see, and I consented to go with him, though I was desirous to re-

visit my friends after an absence of two
years. As we rode through a retired part
of the country, I beheld a school-boy standing
by the side of the road, with his book in his
hand . he kept his eye fixed on something
which the hedge concealed from our sight. I
stopped to know what it might be. ' What
now ?' says my old guide, ' if a red-breast
but flutter in a hedge you must stop come
on, I say, you must derive much amuse-
ment, indeed, from staring a little boy in
the face '——' Pardon me, Sir, I will
alight, I see surprise in the face of the
child, who, seeing me interested also, cried
out, ' look there, Sir.' Close by the shelter
of the hedge, I saw a handsome young man
supporting the head of a dying female , he
seemed to be wholly engrossed by sorrow,
and kissed the pale lips of her who seemed
breathless, crying, ' You are gone, my
sister, your soul, oh ' gentle purity, is on
its wing, and its burden of sorrow is laid
down , may thy guardian angel waft thy
spirit to the highest seat of bliss '' I
waited only to hear the ejaculation finished,

and roused the afflicted youth from his bitter wailing · I felt the pulse of the dying
creature, and found some life ; I gave her
salts to smell, and she heaved a sigh as if
her heart was breaking. I desired the lad
to mount my horse, and go for some assistance. ‘ Alas ! Sir,’ said he, ‘ what can I
do ? it is for want of food that she is so
weak.’ ‘ Is she your wife ?’ ‘ No, Sir,
she is my sister.’ I asked how far it was to
the next town ? ‘ Only a mile, Sir ’—
‘ Well, take my horse, hire a cart, and
bring some cordial, and a little bread and
wine, and I will place your poor sister in
some comfortable asylum before I part with
you. Here is a guinea to get provisions ;
fly, no time is to be lost. I prevailed on
my companion to let me follow the dictates
of the heart on this occasion ; and he assisted
me in raising the drooping head of wretch-
edness indeed no human being could look
on Letty’s situation without sympathy.

‘ Her brother now returned, and bringing
wine, I moistened her lips with it, and she
began to revive. I put a crumb in her

mouth· she swallowed it.—' Come away, now, Sir,' cried my tutor, ' the young woman is better.' ' Well, Sir,' replied I, ' let me only assist in placing her in the cart, and I shall then attend you on your journey.'

' I looked back while this poor young couple were in my sight, and prayed Heaven to comfort them on their way. Next day I was restless, I could not be at ease till I knew their fate, and, as the delay they caused put it out of our power to proceed more than a few miles that night, I returned, alone, in quest of them, and, on enquiring at a small village, I found them. Williams, for that was his name, was preparing some wine-whey, and Letty continued weak, lying on a bed of straw. On my appearance, she coloured like crimson, it was the flush of gratitude I saw it beam in her eyes. ' How is your sister, Sir?' said I ' Extremely weak—I fear she is dying '—Oh ' Sir, she was one of the best of sisters '' The patient now required our attention, for I perceived that Letty was dying. I en-

quired whether she recollected me. ' Yes,'
she replied, ' may Heaven bless thee!'
What a recompence for my feelings,—they
were ten-fold repaid in that blessing! I
own I have often been imposed on, but in
the case of Williams and his sister. I
thought my skill in physiognomy was just,
and I was induced to form the best opinion
of him who called himself her brother. He
was just going to give me some particulars
of his story, when, looking at his precious
charge, and starting up, ' She is gone!' cried he —she raised her languid eyes, and
then closed them for ever!

' I could stay no longer, but gave Williams money enough to enable him to inter
his sister decently, desiring him afterwards
to follow me. He came accordingly, and I
have taken him home. The first night after
his arrival, he gave me the following account
of himself .'

' My sister and I were the children of a
curate in England ; we were born twins —
Our father's whole attention was devoted to
our education, and the important duties of

his avocation, which few ever fulfilled with more devotion or regularity.—Pious, without ostentation —his God and his religion reigned in his heart, and animated his eye. His life was that of purity, and his death, ' the death of the righteous '

' He was of Scotch descent, and married my mother with no other dowery but beauty and innocence —you saw Letty, Sir —She was the exact likeness of her who gave us birth. A legacy falling to my mother some time after her marriage, they thought it most to their advantage to go to England, where the person had lived who bestowed it, hoping that the sister-kingdom might afford more encouragement to a man of my father's talents, but though his endowments were shining, his interest was weak, and he remained many years without even a curacy, but, as yet having no child, their small property supported them.

At length fortune began to dawn on them, and by the interest of a Sir Francis Goodlate, who was appointed trustee of the money bequeathed to my mother by her uncle.

There were three hundred pounds still in Sir Francis's hands, and the year after a curacy was obtained, we blessed them with our entrance into a world that has since afforded us a series of misfortunes.

' As nothing but happiness and peace attended our early days, I may pass them over, till that period which brought our tender parents to the grave My father, at his dying hour, recommended us to the care of Sir Francis, on whose estate he lived , my mother survived but a year after, and, at the tender age of fifteen, we were both orphans, unknowing in the ways of the world. Sir Francis often praised our economy; he said I was an excellent manager, and, in a year or two appointed me his agent, and rendered me many services I had appropriated the money in his hands to the use of Letty.

' We cultivated a neat little garden, and it afforded us plenty The bowers we had planted together were in full perfection at the time we were obliged to quit them for ever , and never did Eve mourn her depart-

ure from Paradise more than Letty did her
garden and peaceful retreat

'Sir Francis cast a licentious eye on my
innocent sister, and became so constant a
visitor at our little dwelling, that she remarked to me, his designs were not good
One day I returned from rowling, and found
Letty in a great fright, she told me a mad-
man came in, and, the maid being out, she
was terrified, but I perceived Sir Francis's
favourite servant leaping over the fence of
our little garden, and knew he had been
sent to visit Letty in my absence Next
day, Sir Francis had the presumption to
make me the horrid proposal, of sacrificing
the honour of my sister to him

'What, Sir,' said I, 'sell an innocent
girl! No, Sir, my sister is as virtuous as
she is fair'——'You are a conceited pup-
py,' said he, 'and I will punish you for
your insolence.' He turned from me, and
my spirit, roused to passion, which I endeavoured to suppress, that I might not
disturb the peace of my sister I returned
to our frugal meal, which Letty never

omitted having ready at my coming. I
could hardly suppress my tears, as I dreaded
the revenge of this seducer.—But my sister's honour was dearer to me than life, and
I afterwards nearly lost it in her defence. I
had hope he would subdue his brutal passion, but, alas! we were doomed to be its
victims. He planned an excuse to send me
out of the way on business, the better to ac-
complish his base resolutions.

' The moment he gave his fatal orders,
something struck my soul of his foul design,
and I lay hid in our little chamber a whole
day, at length the worthless baronet entered our cottage. He enquired if I was returned, and, being answered in the negative,
began to make amorous advances to my sister, and take freedoms that excited my anger.
I endeavoured to subdue my passion, till I
heard him insult her with his offer of taking
her as a mistress. I flew, in a fit of phrenzy,
to a pistol that hung in my room, and discharged the contents at his head. He expired, as we thought, in a few moments.—
We were all in confusion for this rash act of

mine.—We had no alternative but flight or
condemnation , and, leaving our little property behind, exposed ourselves to the
mercy of the world, sooner than be dragged
to prison, and suffer death

‘ We wandered for several days, but
Letty's weak frame was unequal to the hard-
ship of travel, and our finances were nearly
exhausted

‘ A single guinea was the whole of my
purse —we set out early one morning, and,
for the better disguise, exchanged clothes
with my sister   We continued a month in
this state of uncertainty, going from place to
place, and sometimes a corn field received
us for the night, when justice found us a
lodging.   The brother of Sir Francis, no
doubt, offered a reward, and my poor fel-
low-traveller and I were taken and thrown
into prison, from whence we never more
hoped to be set free till death, which I
thought was now inevitable.   I had appli-
cation made to the heir of Sir Francis for
part of our money, and he had the charity
to send us ten guineas,—a seasonable sup-

ply; but what avails the subsistence of the wretch that sees death at hand, and no hope of a release · all my care was for the helpless innocent, my sister. if she obtained her liberty, I feared she would be deprived of her right without my aid; but I committed her most earnestly to our Creator, who knew the purity of her soul. She spent most part of her time in prayer for my liberty. ' Could that be obtained, my brother,' she often exclaimed, ' I should be happy!' One of our fellow-sufferers came to my ward ' Take courage, my lad,' says he, ' this night I will rescue you and your companion from death! The means are in my hands,—be ready at one o'clock, and we shall make the attempt.'

' The hour of deliverance at length came, and we followed the conductor of this enterprize, with the agitation of alternate hope and fear. There were three more in the plot, whom our friend also thought innocent. He first struck off my bolts, and then opened the great lock of our ward.

' We crept along a narrow gloomy passage, and could hear the poor prisoners, in the dungeons below, snoring on their wretched beds, while eternity was at hand with them There was no obstacle in the way of our spirited conductor which he did not get through, and, wrenching off the iron bars of a window, he let down a strong rope, which we held, while he descended by it to the street. In this manner we all descended successively, and in safety.

' Letty's joy for my preservation from death kept up her spirits for some time, but the constant fatigue of travelling, and dread of discovery, affected her health. I thought it best, while I had a little money, to get out of England as speedily as I could. When I came to Wales, Letty fell sick of an ague, and, as I could not get employment, my purse began to exhaust fast, though we lived very sparingly

The horrors of a jail were yet fresh in in Letty's mind, and the noise of the great bolts, and hollow sounds of the dungeon, still rung in her ears Her ague increased, and she became so weak, that I was obliged

sometimes to carry her. I could not get any
employment without a recommendation So
suspicious are the world of strangers, and
my sister still lingering on my hands from
day to day, we were at last obliged
to beg, but without success. Those to
whom I applied told me I was an impostor,
and bade me go and work —When you relieved me, neither my poor sister n r I had
tasted food for two days You know,
Sir, that there is a selfishness in turning
away from the woes of our fellow-creatures,
but you, by bearing a part, lessened mine,
and prov ded a shelter for a dying innocent
to breatl e her last''

'I have the youth at home, ladies,' continued Harris, ' and I think he will not disgrace
me.' The company all said they wished to
see Williams. ' In time you may,' said Harris ' I am very proud of him, I assure you,
I think he will do me credit, I saw integri-
ty in his face, and innocence in that of his
sister —woe to that man who sought to
destroy it '

Harris talked of leaving us.—' Mrs. Fortescue,' said he, ' you ought not to suffer your son to live in this manner. ' It is not my wish,' said she, ' I would gladly see him married, and to one I have long wished, the gentle Harriet.' ' Oh ' then,' replied Harris all is right, for that is done already.' Harriet threw herself on her knees, and begged forgiveness of her mother, and my brother, raising her up, took her by the hand. ' It was I, Madam,' said he, ' that prevailed on this timid fair one to give herself away without your consent, but, you may remember, you long since told me, a partner was growing up for me under your own eye, and the situation our friends have been in for some time past, prevented my making known my happiness : I knew that I had your approbation '' ' Take her, then, my son, and may you both be happy '

' I had often observed that the haughty spirit of Lady Hammond had been mellowed into softness and affability, by the constant society of my mother, whose spirit was all meekness, charity, and love, but affliction, that never-failing guide to him.

lity, and of which she had felt severely by the loss of one darling son, and the infamy of another, might have been the true way of accounting for the change in Lady Hammond's behaviour. Her pride was subdued, and she often confessed to me it required a check.

Lady Hammond, during my residence with her at the castle, ever employed an hour in a manner becoming a rational being; the few months she spent there were only preparatory to the dissipation of London, where a constant round of dress, cards, and other frivolous amusements, occupied the whole of her time. Now, content with such a small circle of society, as her exemplary daughter and our little family afforded, she became a pattern of excellence! She betook herself to religious books!—her charity became universal, and she often declared, that she never knew the value of riches till she became acquainted with Mrs. Fortescue, who was benevolence itself.

A lady of our acquaintance, who had often been assiduous with us in distribution of charity, called on my mother, with a request from Lady Hammond, to come to her immediately, as a female in distress claimed her attention. That was sufficient for my angelic mother! She hastened to relieve, and shortly returned with a beautiful girl, young and dejected, her features were impressed with the traces of sorrow, and in her eyes candour and sensibibility beamed conspicuously. Her figure was delicate, though above the middle size, and her fine brown hair shaded a face, fair though not blooming.—Alas! poor Matilda, tears have worn a furrow in thy cheek, and the rose that was moistened by them, has withered. She complained of excessive weakness, and begged permission to retire to repose. I conducted her to a bed-chamber, and she told me her sleep had been much disturbed for a long period, and that had impaired her intellect. I left her to repose, and, at the expiration of an hour, returning to her bed side, found her still awake.

' Sleep, like the world, his ready visit pays

' Where fortune smiles, the wretched he forsakes,

' Swift on his downy pinions flies from woe,
' And lights on lids unsullied with a tear '

' I hope,' said she, ' you are not uneasy concerning the truth of what Mr Welldone said in my behalf he has given but a slight sketch of my sufferings, and very little to confirm the truth of my not being accessary to the troubles which reduced me to the situation in which you found me. I am not culpable, nor have I been vicious, yet the best of human creatures is imperfect, and, perhaps, for my secret and unknown transgressions, my Creator is pleased to lay his hand on me. I am confident I in some measure deserve it, or I should not have been brought to this, perhaps negligence in my duty, and want of a firm reliance on my God, who alone is the protector of the destitute orphan '—' Commit yourself to his providence,' said I, ' and try to compose yourself you talk too much, Matilda.'— ' Ah !' cried she, ' my spirits are in such a flurry, at this sudden protection from misery, that the joy has overpowered me,' and, throwing her arms around, she grasped me fast, and burst into tears —' Ah! I could sleep here in safety, — I have no enemy here'—Oh! that odious house!—I got a blow on my head — it aches sadly — I wish it were well, and I would tell you all. —See! that ugly woman there again—I cannot forget her — she won't let me sleep— Send for my mother—Oh! all my hopes were blasted when my mother died —Oh! my head! my poor head!'

' I saw no sign of composure in poor Matilda, and consulted with the ladies what to do they came and felt her pulse, and said she was feverish' 'I am, indeed,' said she ' the sudden transition from despair to hope has overpowered my weak frame, but I shall be well by and by '

'We sent for our physician, who prescribed a composing draught, which soon spread its balmy influence over her exhausted frame, and, in a few moments, she fell into a profound slumber.

' She awoke, seemingly refreshed, but her hands were burning, and her face flushed.' 'Oh!" said Lady Hammond, ' I wish

I had kept her to myself; I fear I have brought a fever to your house, my friends ' ' Fear not for us,' said I, ' that good God, whom I trust we serve, by showing compassion on our fellow-creature, will rescue us from any danger that may attend our intentions.' But in three days the afflicted Matilda recovered, and, as she grew strong and composed, gave the following account of herself

' Health, peace, and competence, attended my days, till Heaven deprived me of my parents I was the only daughter of Charles Maywin, a man of singular worth, and my mother was, without exception, a most lovely and virtuous woman. I had four brothers, remarkably handsome men, but fatally addicted to the fashionable vices of the age Our father's attention and economy were not sufficient, at his death, to leave me independent, so embarrassed were his affairs by their repeated extravagancies. My dear mother overlooked their errors, and, at an early age, when vice ought to be curbed by the hand of our

parents, theirs were permitted to obtain un-
controlled sway, and they became the victim of their long-indulged habits. My eldest
brother was a complete country 'squire he
kept hunters and hounds, and the wives and
daughters of our tenantry became his prey.
The younger, as they grew up, followed his
example, till, by their continued extravagance and intrigues, our affairs became too
embarrassed for a man of my father's tender
feelings to bear, without bitter anguish, so
great was his paternal care for his family. At
length he found relief from all worldly care,
by a sudden death, and his successor was a
man ill calculated to fulfil the duties incum-
bent as an elder brother. He, shortly after
my father's decease, separated my mother and
me from him, to live on a jointure, settled
on her at her marriage, and, in a small and
lonely cottage, we lived retired, leaving the
male part of the family to follow without
control the course they had begun. Never-
theless, a separation from her sons was a
heavy affliction to my mother, as she tenderly loved them, but it was the absolute

desire of her first-born Soon after this separation, he married, and got a large fortune, which was soon dissipated, as marriage did, in no degree, confine him within its sacred laws I believe it a just remark, that men, who devote their minds to the grosser appetites, soon became destitute of all the tender ties of friendship and natural affection.

We had the blessing of serenity and retirement—a few friends visited us sometimes · among the male ones was a gentleman of the name of Lesly he and his wife always seemed to have a pleasure in doing us all the little nameless offices of friendship.

My dear mother, though she seldom complained, felt severely the undutifulness of her sons, two of whom left the kingdom with part of the effects my elder brother had shared with them, while the small fortune left me was totally with-held from me by this cruel relative Mr. Lesly, who interested himself in all our affairs, promised to commence a law-suit, to recover my little patrimony, but it was by a tedious process of law, and before it was well begun, my only comfort and support began to droop, and seemed fast falling into the grave.

' The fatal hour at length came, which deprived me of my mother ! From my brother I could expect no protection, the lawsuit against him was commenced, and, had he been amicable before, this circumstance would doubtless have exasperated him. In two days after the death of my mother, who had not seen him for several years, he turned me out of my little cottage ; the land on which it stood being then his own.

Mr. Lesly kindly received me into his house; but I was inconsolable. Wherever I turned my eyes, all was gloomy, sorrowful, and void. The beloved image of my mother appeared to my fancy, and her last agonizing moans still seemed to fill my ears.

' I had not continued long with Mr. Lesly, when I began to find his lady was tired of me. There is a certain delicacy in treating dependants, that few hearts know how to exercise, and the unprotected orphan feels all the rubs incident to that state. This lady was naturally haughty, and selfish, though she had no child to share her fortune

'I had not a relation living of my father's, to whom I could apply for protection. An aunt of my mother's lived in London, whom I remembered when a child. She was rich, but, I suppose, selfish, for she never enquired about us, or our affairs. Lesly and his wife seemed resolved to take me to London with them for some time, and, he, seeing my dejection, one day kindly took my hand, saying, ' I find, Matilda, you are not contended here, on account of my wife's indifference towards you : she wishes to place you with a lady of her acquaintance in town, till I can recover your fortune, and then you may make the best use you can of it, but it is too small to keep you from dependence — Next week,' continued he, ' I shall accompany you to London, but I shall not take my wife with me this time.' ' Accordingly we began our journey, and arrived in London without any remarkable occurrence. Mr. Lesly was all kindness and attention, but, on the second day after our arrival, oh! Lady Hammond, how was I shocked at a declaration of a passion, which he had long indulged, and which, he hoped, I would now reward!' 'I was unable to reply!'—He ordered dinner, and said, he would be back at four, as he was to meet some gentlemen at his house in Grosvenor Square

' He bid me be a good girl, then, going out, left me to the care of his emissary, who, seeing me crying, told me it was all in vain, for her master was determined on detaining me in his own house. ' Let me escape,' said I, 'and I will give you a guinea.' I had but five, as what my mother's little effects amounted to, I had placed in the hands of Mr. Lesly, little suspecting he had even a thought of his late declaration. ' Well,' said the maid, ' if you give me three guineas, I will run the risk of my master's displeasure, and let you go.' The door was lock-

ed.——' See ! here is the key, madam !
—Faith it is a pity to cage a bird that
would rather fly about,— or thing ! have
you been often in London —Don't cry,
—my master is very good to his ladies '—
The hour of Lesly's return approached,
and I was in a state of distraction, not
knowing where to go ——' So, miss,' said
the girl, ' you will stay here to-night, I
see you have no inclination to go. Well,
well, it is a strange thing people don't
know their own minds —there is an old
saying, ' The woman who deliberates is
lost.'

' The wretch took my gold, and showed
me, in return, into the streets of London.
I wandered I knew not whither, and exposed myself, by so doing, to great danger, yet I could not consent to live with
Lesly, my virtuous education forbade it. I
recollected the name of the street where my
aunt lived, but to find it out was to me impossible. A poor woman begged my charity, I told her I would give her something,
if she conducted me to such a street, and

found out the house I wanted. She came most willingly, and, seeing me crying, ' Oh dear !' said she, ' it is no wonder for me to cry, when so fine a lady as you have troubles, I have four small children, and my husband was impressed '—' Have we far to go now ?' said I, being almost exhausted ' Oh ! miss, this is the street '— ' Well, now. find out Mrs Melvin's, and wait for me at the door '—' Oh ! many a bit of meat has her cook given me through these bars,' pointing to the grate ' and now you won't forget the poor children, sweet lady !' ' Stay for me,' said I, ' and, perhaps, you may have me back with you ,' ' O ! mercy, is it home with me ?' ' Yes,' said I, and knocked at the door of my rich relation, when, to my great disappointment, I was told, by an insolent footman, that his lady dined abroad. I begged leave to be admitted, telling him I was a relation, but he bade me leave my name, as it was contrary to custom to let strangers wait ' Well, my lady, where do you want to go now,' said the poor woman, who waited for

me, ' I will do any thing to serve you'
' Take me to your lodgings,' said I, ' and
make haste, that I may get some refreshment, for I am weak and exhausted '
' Ah ! dear, is it to my poor lodgings '
' Yes, I will go with you,—I must wait on
the lady again to-morrow.'—' Well, you
do me great honour to come to my poor
place, and, though it is poor, it is clean,
for I have not been always in a state of po-
verty '

' I was pleased when I arrived at the
place, and, going down a good many steps,
was welcomed by the children, one of whom
got an old chair for me '

' I begged my poor woman would put
down her little kettle, and go buy some tea
and sugar for me, with a loaf of bread I
soon had a frugal meal prepared, and, divid-
ing my loaf with the poor family, I then retired to rest, on a bed of straw, with little
or no covering ' It was clean, for I got the
poor woman to buy it fresh, and she and
her little family gave me the bed they lay

on themselves, making another on the floor by my side.

'Nature being quite exhausted, I fell asleep, and did not awake till the morning showed me my wretched situation! Oh! Lesly, what a heart is yours! and to what misery have you reduced me!—Oh! it was cruel!

'I recollected that my travelling trunk was left at the inn, on our arrival in town, and I desired my kind hostess to go and demand it I had some fears for its safety, thinking Lesly would send for it, as a means of my applying to him, and once more getting me into his power, but so far I had fortune on my side, that I saw my clothes arrive safe, and was so well pleased, that I sent out for a bit of meat for dinner : before it was dressed, there entered a good-looking man, in the habit of a sailor, the poor woman almost fainted, while he caught her in his arms. 'Ah! my dearest Billy !' cried she, 'is it you!—is it you!—where have you been this wearisome time from your wife and little ones?' ' You know I could not come, Nancy,' said he; ' all my care has been for you and your little children.—How have you existed?'

' This happy man was so intoxicated with the joy of coming home, that he could scarce perceive a stranger; and when he cast his eyes on me, he looked inquisitively, and I heard him ask, ' Who is that lady?' ' Oh!' returned his wife, ' that lady is an angel! for she has relieved us, and given the children and me as much as we could eat.' ' Well, my Nancy, you shall never beg again while I have health to earn you bread!' ' But tell me, Billy, how did you escape, after being shipwrecked?' ' All perished but five and myself, who, with hard buffeting against the waves, and the help of a plank, got on shore!' ' I'm sure you are a blessed creature,' says the poor woman to me, ' for you brought me comfort I little expected! but we had better eat our bit of dinner '—She laid mine on a stool, and a little clean apron of one of the children for a cloth, to show her respect, the rest of the

family went all together to a little table —
Billy had money, and sent out for beer to
drink all our healths   After this refreshment, we thanked that bountiful hand that
fed us

   ' I dressed again in the afternoon, to visit
my aunt. and, taking my guide along with
me, once more entered her great hall, and,
finding she was at home, I bade my poor
woman farewell, and desired her to come next
day at one o'clock, and I should speak to her
concerning my trunk   Not knowing what
reception I might meet with from my aunt,
I thought I might be glad of the cellar again
for shelter   My heart palpitated with anxiety, lest I should not be well received by this
lady, when the footman showed me into the
parlour   I had not strength to speak. but,
recovering myself before she made her appearance, was somewhat composed, when
the door opened, and a stiff old figure entered the room   I took my mother's picture from my breast, and, showing it, said,
it would introduce me to her better than I
could.   ' Well, child, and you tell me your

mother is dead,—well, and what brought
you to London ?' ' Distress, madam "
' Well, then, it is the worst place in the
world for distressed people to come to I
wonder you did not try to stay in the country, poor thing " I said, if she would per-
mit me, I would tell her a story, which
would account for all my conduct

' I related Lesly's cruel designs, but
saw very little appearance of its melting her
heart in my favour. I thought she looked
at me with suspicion. I told her I would
gladly earn my bread, if she would recommend me to some place ' Why, as to
that,' said she, ' gentlewomen find it most
difficult to be useful, what can you under-
take to do ?—You were not bred a servant,
and you cannot do laborious work, if you
had a taste for dress, I do not doubt but
I might want you myself, for my present
maid does not know how to dress my hair,
or put on my clothes to advantage, but she
is an excellent girl for all that, and I cannot part with her. I suppose you can read
well ?' I told her I could. and would en-

deavour to please her to the utmost of my abilities, if she would but give me her sanc tion, even for a short time. ' Well,' said she, ' I am to have company to tea and supper, you may go sit in my room, and amuse yourself with a book, or work, and I will consider of this matter ' My feelings were hurt by her ill-natured manner . I expected so near a relation of my mother would have embraced me , but cold and indifferent was my reception.

' Her waiting-woman came to the apartment where I sat, and cast on me a look of jealous contempt! She eyed me inquisitively, and asked some impertinent questions, which I answered civilly. We drank tea together, and she gave me to understand, her mistress set a high value on her —— I thought I never saw so ill-favoured a woman, and she excited a kind of fear in me not to be described. My aunt sat up late with her company, and the next morning went a visiting, and dined abroad. I had little of her company for the first week, and Mrs. Deborah was not in-clined to make herself agreeable to me. I did some work for my aunt, which she liked very well, and I read to her. She praised my manners and education, and, I believe, but for the imbecility which made her a dupe to the arts of her woman, she might have proved a kind relation.

When she favoured me with her company, she told me, if she could stay at home I would be a pleasure to her, but so numerous was her acquaintance, she must be among them, and would try to get me a place as waiting-maid to some lady. ' Do not tell any one you are my relation,' said she ' I fear my woman has got a hint of it —she has been with me near twenty years; she is a good creatu ?' I do not believe a word of that, said I to myself, I perceived the foible of my aunt was, the love of praise, and this woman flattered her continually, by telling her, that she looked as young and handsome as when she was but twenty, and how well that cap became her '—how genteel that gown looked on her' She wondered Mr. Such-a-one was not here to-day,

———Believe me, madam, he is wretched about you!" I could not but smile at so inconsistent a piece of deceit, for my aunt was old, and had not the smallest remains of beauty. I felt for her weakness, in suffering such a creature to flatter her.

' I had now lived a week with my aunt, and thought she was growing kind to me, which. created so much envy in Mrs Debby, that she put a plan in execution to deprive me of the shelter of the roof this base woman put a necklace of my aunt's into my trunk, which my poor woman brought me the day after I came. There were several things also missing in the house, which my aunt began to make a great noise about, hinting at me, who, feeling the insult, got a prayer-book in my hand, and, falling on my knees before her, swore, in the most solemn manner, that I was innocent of the knowledge of the smallest matter she had lost! ' You are a perjured wretch!" said she ' let me search your trunk instantly, and I shall find my necklace.' I brought it

to her, and she took out my clothes, one
by one, when, behold ' to my great confusion, in the bottom was found the necklace, and a silver spoon, rolled up in paper'
I was ready to faint, and could not say a
word ‘ You are now completely detected,’
said my aunt ‘ your fine story of Mr. Lesly
was all false, you are a vile wretch,—begone out of my house —it is to a prison you
ought to be sent, as a punishment for your
treachery ’

‘ She then threw open the street door,
and I was obliged once more to seek refuge
in the old cellar, where my poor woman received me with open arms ‘ Oh ' my poor
lady ' those relations are very bad to one in
distress '— It is a strange world '— Oh!
dear' dear' how could she have the heart to
serve you so ?' I sent her immediately for
my trunk, and, as my little money was
nearly exhausted, I foresaw I should be
obliged to sell part of my clothes

‘ When the poor woman came back, she
said she had been thinking, as she went
along, of my applying to a very charitable

clergyman, who lived in the neighbourhood
and that she would show me the place to-
morrow. This hope cheered me a little:
and, with the pleasing idea of a kind reception next day, I sent out for my dinner.
' Will you take a bit of my bread?" said the
good-natured woman, ' I never wanted since
you first visited me ; you brought home my
Billy, and all has gone well since.'

' Next morning I was conducted to the
clergyman's house by my poor friend,
and asked admittance to the divine, who
soon made his appearance, and showed me
into a parlour off the hall. I told him, in
the most simple manner, my situation, so
totally unprotected, that I was willing to
earn my bread, if I could find the means of
doing so ' He abruptly answered, that he
would have nothing to do with a stranger.
' Where did you come from, young woman?" said he. ' From the country, Sir.'
' Well, I would have you go back again
where you are known , I shall have nothing
to do with you, so it is in vain for you to
take up my time any longer.'

' I departed with an aching heart, and almost despaired of the mercies of my Creator ' I gave myself over for lost and saw no prospect of hope.——Even had I been in possession of money, I should have been afraid to venture into any other lodgings alone, but that was not the case, for my last shilling was expended. I wept bitterly, and my poor companion did all she could to comfort me. Her husband came in, and found me weeping. ' Come, cheer up, miss,' said he, ' blubbering will not avail in a storm !' ' Oh !' replied I, ' I am a miserable creature !' ' Heaven will yet raise you up a friend,' said he ' Perhaps, Billy,' said his wife, ' it was a wrong place I took her to, for every one talks of the goodness of that man I wonder he did not take compassion on her, and give her something ' ' I will lay my life you steered a wrong course ' ' It was to parson R——'s I went,' said she ' I knew you foundered on a rock, for that man's heart is as hard as one, he never did a good action in his life it was to Mr. Welldone's you ought to have gone,—he lives in this very street, and, though not half so rich as R———, he does more good in a week than the other has done all his life' for if he can keep free from danger, he cares not though he sees his messmates sinking ' ' Well, to-morrow, we will go to Mr Welldone,' said his wife So I committed myself to Heaven for that night.

' We went next day, to try what success I might have with Mr. Welldone , but, on enquiring at the door for him, were in-formed he was gone to the country for a few days Now, thought I, every effort has failed me, and I must famish.' ' Come home, dear lady,' said my poor guide Sad was my heart, at the words, ' come home'' Alas! I had no home, or kindred,—a wretched outcast

Oh' cruel Lesly' that betrayed me thus, —how could your base heart form such de-signs ?—I looked up to you for protection, and you would ruin me ——Well might he know, from the virtuous principles in which I had been educated, that I would not receive his guilty proposals , Oh' no,

though death should be the result, but I
find it is not near to ease me of my wearisome existence! In this situation I remained for a week, enquiring often for Mr.
Welldone, who, I at last heard, was returned, and my poor woman brought me
this intelligence on her return home from
the pawnbroker's, where she had been getting money to buy me necessaries. She also told me, that a fine young gentleman had
stopped her in the street, and enquired who
that pretty girl was she was walking after
yesterday? 'He said he would give me a
guinea, if I would show him where to find
you, but I would scorn to take it without
first letting you know, and who knows,
my young mistress, but he may mean well,
and make your fortune' 'Oh!' said I, 'it
was with a motive to be free from such im-
pertinence, that I preferred your humble
lodgings, take care you have not betrayed
me.' 'Not I,' said she, 'I would not do
any thing to disoblige you for the world,
and, if I did, it would be only with a good
intent' She went out next morning, and I

desired her to be soon back, that I might go
to Mr. Welldone. I was sitting alone, with
a heavy heart and an aching head, rumi-
nating on all my miseries, when down the
cellar steps came a fine powdered coxcomb
' I am sorry, madam, to see a lady of your
appearance in such a place as this , if my
services can be in the smallest degree useful, you may command them.' I told him
I would accept of no services from him, and
begged he would intrude no longer on
which he drew near, and began to be quite
familiar, offering to take my hand, and use
liberties, I in vain tried to suppress. My
landlord coming in at that instant, I desired
him to turn the fellow out, for he had insulted me. The honest man took a cudgel
from a corner, and gave the beau a stroke
on the back and another on the head.—He
was glad to make the best of his way out,
leaving me in the utmost terror , as I was
very weak before, this left me in a state of
perturbation. The anger, which appeared
in the face of my honest host, was not to
be described ; and, only in pity to me, he

would have given the intruder a more severe chastisement; but I was so terrified, that he let him pass into the street, where he said he had sea-room enough, not to run foul of honest people.

' When my landlady returned, I censured her very much for what she had done, but she protested she meant no harm, thinking it might turn out well, and that he might marry me. She owned she had taken the guinea, and had brought home some provisions for it, seeing I was not taking proper nourishment. She wished to have me take something good, and had brought home some cakes, and other nice things, to tempt me to eat; and, offering me the change, I refused it, saying, I never would touch a halfpenny of it. ' I fear you are angry with me, my young mistress,' said she, ' I would not vex you for the world, I thought the youth might be in love with you. I'm sure I would not, for the world, do it again; but I had good hopes from it: however, since he behaved so rudely, I am glad he got what he deserved.' ' I will go

to see Mr. Welldone to-day,' said I. 'Do,
and may God incline his heart to do you good.
I'm sure I am not tired of your company,
but this is a sad place for you to be in, lying
on a straw bed oh! dear! dear! but it is a
pity to see it!—Oh! don't look so sorrowful, miss!' 'I must look so,' said I, 'for
grief has taken full possession of my heart'

'I took some refreshment, and tried once
more to assume courage to go to Mr Welldone's I had the good fortune to find him at
home, the sight of him raised my languid
spirits to a dawn of joy, he brought me into
a neat parlour, and looked, I thought, as
though he had already relieved me. I could
read in his benign countenance hope and
consolation He listened to my story, while
I related every circumstance, and told him,
but for the base Lesly, I should never have
ventured to London without some recommendation, but, relying on his promises
and interest, I sought no other. Mr. Welldone's advice to me was, to write immediately to some reputable person, who could
authenticate my story, after which some-

thing should be done for me ——'I do believe you speak truth,' said he, 'keep up your spirits, and trust in your God, who will deliver you in his good time, out of all your sufferings. For my part,' continued this pattern of benevolence, though I have but very little to bestow on the distressed, I have it in my power to speak to those who can protect them. He put a guinea in my hand, saying, 'Poor soul! you look the picture of woe! so young, and seemingly so innocent, hard has been thy portion, and thy years as yet but few, however, I trust the worst is past come to me to-morrow, but tell me now where you lodge.' I told him.—'Oh! that is a sad place, poor girl, yet, perhaps, it is safer than a better.' I told him I could not afford a better, as I had but three guineas in my pocket when I was turned into the streets.

'I prayed Heaven to bless my benefactor, and, that the short ray of joy he had conveyed to my tortured bosom, might be tenfold rewarded hereafter. He bade me a tender farewell at the door, desiring me to to come next day, and he would introduce me to his wife.

' When I returned to the cellar, I threw myself on my knees, and raised my eyes to Heaven, in thanks for the relief it had be-stowed. If Mr. Welldone never does more for me, thought I, but treating my misfor-tunes with kindness, he has done me good.

' Pity is one attribute of Heaven,' said Mrs. Fortescue, ' they who treat misfortunes unfeelingly, deserve not the name of Chris-tians. Our great Master and Patron was a man of sorrow and acquainted with grief, and, for his sake, every child of sorrow is dear to my heart;—but go on with your story, Matilda. I know the worth of Mr. Welldone, you are not the first he has pro-cured shelter for · if he had as hard a heart as the first you applied to, you had been ere this lost, my poor girl ''

' Ah ! madam,' continued Matilda, ' I should have been lost and undone but for him; but for him, I should have sunk in endless misery ; but you shall hear ·

' As I was returning to him the next

day, I was stopped by the very man who
came to visit me in the cellar, and a carriage immediately drawing up close to me,
with the blinds up, he placed me in it, and
conveyed me to a house, of what kind you
may easily imagine. He introduced me to
some fine ladies there, and withdrew. I
now saw no hopes of a rescue from a life I
had endeavoured to avoid. These gawdy
figures were adorned with all the costly plu-
mage of modern taste · an old dowager desired I should be taken up stairs, and dress
quickly, as they expected some company to
supper.——' What ails you, miss?—why
do yo look so sad?—Go dress—you are so
pretty, you will cut us all out of feather'
—Go up, miss, directly,—don't delay.
She drew near me, and the smell of li-
quor was as strong as if she had just come
from a brandy cask she was really drunk,
and I made her no kind of reply Expos-
tulation I thought would be vain with such
a hardened wretch, she took me by the
hand, which I withdrew instantly, and
thinking herself offended, she gave me a

blow on the head, which stunned me completely, and left me, for some minutes,
unconscious of my dreadful situation. I
complained of the hurt, and, laying my
head on a sofa in the room, seemed more
dead than alive. The wretch who had used
me thus, began to relent, and beg of me to
forgive her, saying, she was a little pas-
sionate, but had no harm in it, and that she
would be very fond of me for the future.
' You shall have every thing your heart can
wish for;' said she, ' fine clothes and car-
riages to go out in, in short, every thing a
fine lady can desire ' But it seems Heaven
designed me not for such misery, for, as this
vile woman was speaking thus, two gentlemen made their appearance. One of them
said, ' The lady has been forced here, and
we must rescue her.' Joy overwhelmed me
at the sound, and, oh ! think, madam, how
I was amazed and delighted, to behold my
guardian angel in the person of Mr. Well-
lone ! I threw myself on my knees, and
implored his protection. He raised me up,
and taking me under the arm, the other

gentleman followed with a pistol in his hand, and a sword by his side we passed unmolested through this abode of demons he had a carriage at the door, in which he placed me not a soul dared to molest us. So here was I once more released by that all-protecting and all-powerful hand, which guards the innocent, and being tenderly received by Mrs. Welldone, was put to bed, extremely weak from the blow I had received on my head, and from which I felt exquisite pain

'Mr. Welldone, when he found I did not come, as he desired me, to his house, went to enquire for me, where I had told him I lodged the honest people were truly alarmed, and told Mr. Welldone I was worthy of his compassion, being one of the best behaved young women they ever saw ' 'Oh! what is become of her?' said the poor woman, ' for she went out to go to your house.' ' I will lay my life,' said her husband, ' I shall find her, stay but a moment, Sir, I am certain it was her, since she is not with you '

'The man returned in a short time, with a fellow-tradesman of his, who gave the following account, that he saw a young woman just at the end of the street, forced into a carriage · she was crying so bitterly, that he pitied her, and got behind it, unknown to the driver   It stopped at a noted house of ill fame, where a gentleman took her out in his arms, and carried her in almost dead with fear!'   'Oh! it was her, sure enough,' said the poor woman, 'she would not go the length of the street without some one with her, but that your house was so near, Sir. Oh! poor thing, she is lost.'   'She shall not be lost,' said this best of men , and, flying home, called on a friend, who came with him to my deliverance.

'You know the rest, ladies, you have brought me back from the grave, and Mr. Welldone from endless misery !   The merit of your beneficence is its own reward, I have nothing to bestow but prayers and gratitude '

We daily had the pleasure of seeing poor Matilda recover fast, and getting a certificate from the family she had written to concerning her former conduct, which was irreproachable, relating the vile conduct of her brother, with regard to her, and the best of mothers, this, from a family of respectability in Devonshire, who knew Matilda's circumstances, and did not vary from her own account, gave us infinite pleasure, and we were amply requited for our trouble, by finding the object so worthy.

I need not trouble my reader with any trifling occurrences, that happened in our family for two succeeding years, unless the birth of a son, to my dear brother, which caused great joy. There had not been any account from Lord George since the dreadful catastrophe. He flew from his country, like a muderer, and had not since been heard of. Soon after the birth of young Fortescue, my brother took a house, and went to reside in it, much to the affliction of us all ; but it was in our neighbourhood, and Mrs. Harris removing her family to town, we all lived in the most perfect amity, till two events took place that broke the happy connection

Lady Hammond's health had hourly declined since the fatal event, which robbed her of her son The jaundice seized her, and she was not long attacked with it when my amiable Charlotte was left without a mother As she was the first friend I ever knew, I felt nearly as much sorrow as her daughter. My mother was much affected with the death of her friend, but her own time was near drawing to a conclusion, and she survived her friend but one year Her final scene was conformable to a life spent in holiness, and she expired as like an angel as she had lived, requesting Charlotte and I would never part, and, blessing all around her, she resigned her last breath without a pang

One of Lord George's agents came to town, soon after my dear mother's death, to pay off some arrears due to Charlotte — He said his master was in Germany, and that he had ordered him to let Hammond Castle This did not show any intention of

returning, and was a means of fowarding
our plan, to live in a country place, where
our eyes might once more behold the beauties
of nature, when we retired from the busy
scenes of a city A country seat was soon
found to our wish, within three miles of London. Harris, and his favourite Williams,
were also busily employed in our removal.

The reader will remember Williams, he
appeared a fine lad, and, when first introduced to our family, we thought on a match
between him and Matilda, who was to make
one of our household The youth became
much enamoured with Matilda's charms,
but not knowing our intention, pined in
secret Harris insisted on knowing the
cause, and Williams could conceal nothing
from his kind benefactor he confessed a
passion which he strove to conquer, knowing, circumstanced as he was, he could not,
with propriety, marry 'Why not, my
boy'' said the generous youth, ' you, or
your wife, shall never want, I will let you
a farm, and lend you money to stock it.—

I am sure the ladies will make up some
of money for Matilda, and we shall have
the pleasure of setting up our Devonshire couple in housekeeping, so I shall pro-
pose for you, Williams, and get you the
wife.'

Accordingly, Harris broke the affair to
Charlotte and me, begging our intercession
with Matilda ; he said we could not bestow
her better, or on a more worthy lad : ' they
are both well born, and, I think, for each
other too. I shall make a proposal, which, if
you agree to, we shall have the match made
directly with Matilda's consent. If you
will give the girl a little money, I shall
settle Williams comfortably so, let me hear
what you say, ladies, I must see Williams
happy — his heart is engaged to Matilda,
and I hope she will reward him.'

' We both laughed at the warmth of
Harris's disposition, and thought, if Matilda would consent, it would be desirable
on both sides. Miss Hammond promised
two hundred pounds, and I, not having so

large a fortune as Charlotte, was to give one, with some furniture.

Now all that was wanting to complete the business, was the lady's consent, and Williams was the fittest to gain that He slily took every opportunity of showing her his prepossession—all was soon agreed on, and a day fixed for the wedding. Harris was beside himself with extacy, and he gave the pretty blushing Matilda to his favourite Williams. Never was joined a pair more suitable for each other, as both had been tried in the school of adversity, and suffered for virtue's sake.

' We could not part with the young couple until our removal from town, as their assistance was wanting, and Williams was an excellent and ingenious young man for planning and improving we took him and his fair bride to the country with us. A description of our retreat would be too tedious to give in full, as it surpassed our own ideas, till we saw it. There were flowery lawns, purling streams, romantic bowers, and trees in great profusion. The house stood on a rising ground, but was so shaded as not to be visible till we entered the outward gate. The gardens all in order, and every flower of the spring, blooming in the fullest perfection.

From the death of my dear mother I wished to quit our house in London, every place there reminded me of her, and when alone, and thinking of her, a kind of stupor took possession of me. Charlotte felt much the same way, so we hoped to enjoy more tranquillity in our rural habitation. We brought all our old domestics with us, and found ourselves comfortably situated.

Nothing remarkable happened for two years after our removal to our country house. We were blessed in each other's society, and the services of our faithful Williams and Matilda were too essential to our happiness to part with them, for some time longer, though Harris was anxious to settle them in a house of their own.

Our time was occupied in a variety of delightful amusements, and our solitary walks were not less pleasing. When mus-

ing on past scenes, and on the memory of
dear departed friends, we lost ourselves in
meditation Oh! Edwin, thou best of men!
how often have I indulged my thoughts to
dwell on thy matchless perfections!

One fine summer's evening, as Charlotte and I were sauntering in a thick recess
of the wood, a shadow passed, which we
thought bore the resemblance of our dear departed Edwin. We persuaded ourselves it
was only fancy, and walked into a little
grotto, which we no sooner entered, than
the soft sounds of music charmed our ear.
At a distance it was sweet beyond concep-
tion, and seemed the sound of two flutes
in perfect unison. 'Well, Charlotte,' said
I, 'something extraordinary is come to
visit us in our retreat' We walked towards the house, the sounds following till
they died away on the evening breeze The
birds caught the soft melody, and sung re-
sponsive. We began to feel a little alarmed,
and still thought on the glimpse we had of
something like the form of Edwin. His
stature, his look, in short, we both agreed

it was like him, and, again, set it down for nothing but mere fancy, because we had been talking of him, and our minds were filled with the idea. We reached the house, and sent Williams, with two more of our men, to look about the improvements, and try if they could hear the music again; but it was heard no more, and no human creature was to be seen. On the following afternoon we ventured out again, when the evening flies were on the wing, and the hum of the bee led us on to the same grotto. We sat attentively listening, but no music returned to our ear, or shadow passed our eye, till, at length, we almost persuaded ourselves we had not seen it, and with that idea returned home. We disposed ourselves for bed, and our chamber window looking into that part of the wood, we listened attentively, with the sash open, and distinctly heard the same sweet notes, but they soon stopped, and left us in wonder at again hearing them! We could get little repose that night, for this extraordinary adventure of the music's returning again, agitated us, and alarmed Charlotte even more than me, but this was trifling to what followed.——Williams returned one evening with terror in his looks, after he had been viewing his flocks and plains, and told us a gentleman lay, weltering in his blood, in a ditch by the road side ; and as there was no house within a mile of us, asked our permission to assist the distressed man. he said he had got one wound in his breast, and, when he asked him how it happened, was told, it was by robbers, who fired at him, and took his purse, watch, and pocket-book. We trembled at the idea of letting him into the house; yet, as it was night, to have a fellow-creature dying without a roof to shelter him, humanity shrunk from it, and we consented to let him be carried in. Williams got a door for the purpose, and called help. It was a solemn and alarming moment, and struck such terror into our breasts, that we could not rest all night. Charlotte or I could not look at the dying man, and only assisted with directions, such as we thought most wanting.

A surgeon was with him in a quarter of an hour after being sent for, and the wound was dressed A high fever ensued, in which the ravings of the patient were dreadful. Charlotte and I attempted to go look at the poor sufferer, but on coming to the door, hearing him rave so wildly, we withdrew again.

In a few hours after we returned, and approached as far as the bed, but could not get a glimpse of his face, the room being dark, and he lying with his back to us. We heard him say distinctly, ' I must go—Oh! I am a villain '—My God '—it is too late now—Who is there ?——See that ghost '—how it stalks—it comes for me—I am not ready—not ready yet—Oh '——,

' Charlotte,' said I, ' are not these dreadful ravings, come away, oh! come away, my love ' we will send for Harris to come and relieve us in this our distress it is trying my fortitude too much. He owns he has been a villain, that word alarms me beyond all the rest. He, no doubt, is one of the highwaymen—what shall we do with him ?'

' Nothing, my dear Emma,' said Charlotte.
' but let him die, and what injury can that
do us ? I would have a clergyman sent for.
as he really wants peace of mind. I will
send for Mr. Welldone directly ' ' It is in
vain, my dear,' replied I, ' till his fever is
abated, as he is now delirious, besides, his
torture is so great, he could not listen
with composure to any advice '—but let
us watch the moment when the poor sinner can be spoken to We shall visit
him in the evening. Williams says his
face is all swelled, and that he is certain
he is a gentleman, by the fineness of his
hands, and his whole appearance ' ' God
comfort him !' exclaimed honest Williams,
' he is in sad despair ' Poor soul ' he
asked me last night whose house he was in,
and, being told, he soon after raved of
indifferent matters, trying to get out of
bed, and starting so violently, he terrified me too much to stay alone again
with him Two men sat up each night
he remained in this situation, for ten

days, and no signs of his recovery appeared

While matters were in this train, a stranger arrived, whom, though I knew not, Charlotte had once been interested in, and he now came to offer her that heart and hand, which should have been hers, but for a former engagement, which honour forbade him to break. At sight of Henry, the friend of Edwin, my heart was wrung, and Charlotte was not a little embarrassed. ‘ Henry is now at liberty,’ said I, ‘ and will my Charlotte part with her Emma '—Yes, she will ' the ties and promises we formed, are now broken , and let the happiness of my friend, recompense me for her loss.— Go, my Charlotte, and be happy with thy Henry, who is come to break the sweet tie that linked our hearts together.’——‘ Not so fast, my friend,’ cried she, ‘ let not thy fears disturb thee , I would not part you for the world’s wealth , my fixed and unalterable resolution is, to live single, and with you to end my days, in that sacred

bond, which unites two hearts in the purest affection ! What ! leave my Emma ?
—No—leave the beloved of Edwin without
her better half '—it must not—shall not be !'

' Harris arrived soon afterwards, which
pleased us much, as he would be company
for Henry, and, the house being all in confusion, the gentlemen made us easy by their
protection , and as there was no hope of
the sick man's recovery, we committed him
wholly to our male friends Harris had
not yet seen him , and as I also wished it,
we got a candle, and, finding him in a
slumber, held it to view his face, when,
oh ! what were my feelings, on beholding
the cause of all my sorrows, and the murderer of my Edwin ? Harris could not support me — I fainted away — Charlotte and
Henry came in, and, alarmed, asked the
cause of my illness. Charlotte, looking
inquisitively in my face, ' What ails my
Emma ?' ' Look there,' I cried, ' look,
there he lies ! Oh ! to what strange events
is my life exposed ? I thought all was past,

and the remainder of my days had nothing more to afford surprise, but this is too much!' 'Who is it?' asked Charlotte, 'I do not know him, do you, Emma?' 'Oh! yes, I know him too well—would I could conceal him from you, but I cannot—— it is thy brother—the unhappy source of all our troubles!—it is Lord George, my Char - lotte, that lies before you!' 'Gracious powers! Oh! Lord George! unhappy man! are you come to lay down a life of wicked- ness with those you have endeavoured to in- jure? Unhappy man! will mercy dawn upon you?—Are you come, with sincere repentance, to get forgiveness from her you have so often afflicted?'

We could scarcely hear him answer — 'Yes'— 'If he answers, I will speak to him,' said Harris, 'it is fit he should be spoke to, let us try what he has to say, perhaps his senses are restored' He answered again, 'They are!—Am I in Emma Fortescue's house?' 'Yes, and in your sister's too.'

Emma, will you forgive me, and pray

for a penitent sinner' I have much to say, and much more to do. Oh! if I had strength to tell you——Support me in the bed, that I may speak to you all before I die!—Oh! it is a long journey!—Come away—see that ghost again, how it stalks! —'tis all in glorious apparel!—Blessed spirit, come not near a wretch!'

Thus he raved by starts, and again slumbered The surgeon came, and probed his wound afresh, he said, he judged it would prove mortal After the exquisite torture it put him to in the dressing, he fell asleep, and, on waking, sent for us, saying, he was now in his perfect senses, and would make use of them, in begging our prayers, and forgiveness, for all his past offences

'I have,' said he, 'been in London these three months past, and often came about this house at different hours,—not with that base intent I once harboured, but with heart-felt sorrow, and wishing some means might offer to be reconciled to my sister and Miss Fortescue, whom I have so often injured On my return from the wood, where I have frequently roved about, without daring to approach the house, I received this fatal wound which is about to put an end to my mortal career. Oh! had I lived retired from the vices of a vain world! the arrows of remorse would not sting me thus, and the happy spirit of Edwin, my brother, would not call for vengeance of his blood, but his gentle spirit is too mild for reproach!

' A robber attacked me, and, after giving me the fatal wound, escaped I made my will as soon as a reformation began to dawn upon me, and bequeathed my estate to those I have so much injured in my life What first roused me from sin, was a beautiful lady, who freely consented to live with me, shortly after Miss Fortescue made her escape On the recovery of the illness she left me in at London, I set out for Naples. Shortly after I returned again to London, with a diabolical plan for your undoing, much-injured Emma There was not a change in your circumstances, that

I was not made acquainted with from time to time, my correspondents telling me you had discovered your mother, and were going to be married to Edwin, I took revenge, fatal revenge, and returning to the Neapolitan lady, lived in luxury and wickedness, stifling the pangs of conscience for the murder of my amiable brother, for this dissipated woman would not give me time to think. She was so far right, for my own thoughts were my worst enemies ——But I can say no more—lay me back—Oh! my tortured breast "—Lord George was exhausted, and, taking a drink, fell asleep, from thence he began to rave and start, wanting to get out of bed. Charlotte and I left the unhappy man to the care of the gentlemen, and withdrew to rest. We continued in a state of langour, thinking on the awful event that must shortly take place, and Charlotte requested to have a clergyman brought to him next morning.

The servant came to our door, and begged us to go down, as the gentlemen thought Lord George showed certain symptoms that he could not live till morning we found him convulsed, and the cold damps of death seemed coming on Towards day he grew easier, and took some cordial, he fell asleep again leaving Williams and his Matilda to watch, we went to bed, and did not awake till one o'clock the same day.

On going into the sick man's room, we found Williams supporting him · he was still able to speak ' I would fain give you every satisfaction while life remains,' said he ' I know that the cold hand of death is on me, I will own to you, that I laid many plans to be admitted to this house, and get forgiveness, but dared not put any of them in execution. I feared to meet so much virtue and merit, convinced of my unworthiness. I have written some letters, which I did not venture to send; but the assassin has got admittance for me, and if I can get forgiveness for my past offences, I shall thank the hand that gave the blow.' ' Our forgiveness you have, Lord George,' we replied, ' seek it from him who has a right to punish.' We asked him to admit

Mr. Welldone, who was sent for. He said he would, and begged we would all join in prayer, for Heaven to forgive him. We asked him concerning the Neapolitan lady, who, he told us, had first given him a disgust to the life he was following He said he was passionately attached to her, and thought she was equally so to him His purse was drained by her extravagance ·
' But one day, happening to return home at a time she did not expect me, I found a French Count sitting in her lap ——this fired me with jealousy, yet I thought it most prudent to wait till I could detect her farther. I had just got in rents from my agent, and putting four bank notes in my poket-book, to the amount of sixteen hundred pounds, never once upbraided my mistress with her want of fidelity I came home the following night, much intoxicated, and slept till twelve next day, when, behold, all my notes, and many other valuable articles, with my fair mistress, were gone I heard she and the paramour I had found

with her, were gone to travel, no one knew whither.

The infidelity of one, I had such confidence in, first opened my eyes, and I hope my Creator inspired my heart with repentance. I then thought of returning home, and making you and my family some reparation for all the wrongs I had done them.'

The repentant sufferer excited our compassion I exerted my abilities to speak peace to his troubled conscience, drew near him at all times of his returning reason, assuring him, from my heart, of my forgiveness, and telling him with sincerity, that my prayers should be offered up for his reconciliation with Heaven ! 'You are, Lord George,' said I, ' in a fair way for it already , you feel you are humbled, and now, returning grace may find favour, through the merits of him who is mercy itself Mr. Welldone is come—shall I call him?" ' Do,' said the dying man, ' and let him pray !" I shall never forget the solemn scene ! We all assembled round the bed, and that exemplary divine performed his office with true devotion! The dying penitent, with eyes and heart lifted up to heaven, sought the balm of consolation, and seemed composed. Mr Welldone came again in the afternoon, I asked him, if he had any hopes of a recovery. He said he had none It was a dreadful and an alarming period, his much afflicted sister and I could ill support it. Each hour seemed drawing towards the final close of this unhappy man The surgeon thought he might linger out a week longer. At the dressing his wound his agony was extreme, yet he complained of much greater in his soul! ' Youth,' said he, ' is the season to gather the fruit, I have been a negligent husbandman, and let the weeds grow up till they exhausted the soil.' ' Let not despair again overtake thee,' said I, ' it is dangerous to indulge it; you were in a right train of thought some hours ago, continue to persevere and hope, with humble confidence, in thy Saviour's blood ' ' Oh! thou angel,' cried he, ' thou comforter! thou art doing good for all the wrongs I have heaped on thee, wrongs not to be equalled, I feel them all—they are now on this wretched head. Oh! my head is full of wrongs—Will the good man come to-night?" I asked who he meant. 'Mr. Welldone,' said he We sent a dispatch instantly for him, but before his return Lord George had fainted away, and we thought he had resigned his breath, but his bountiful Creator restored him again to recollection and penitence He called us all round his bed 'Where are you, my friends?—Oh! that I had deserved you!—When I am no more—think sometimes of him—who, if he could again live over his days, would live in rectitude. Oh! Edwin, I would listen to all thy wise counsels, and treasure them in my heart!—but now it is too late '—— 'No, Lord George, it is not, do not again despair, your heart is contrite, you feel a humble sense of your situation, and I trust will obtain pardon.' 'Blessed comforter!" again he replied, and seemed growing faint. We gave him some medicine, and left him seemingly in an easy slumber, with Williams and his gentle Matilda in the room. The clock struck four, and dinner being served, we attempted to eat, but it was only an effort Henry used his utmost exertions and attention to comfort Charlotte : never was a more awful scene than that which lay before us, a desponding sinner, going to launch into the great abyss of eternity; and well might he say with Cato, that

' Shadows, clouds, and darkness rest upon it.'

Williams came down to tell us he was in an easy sleep, but sometimes talked to himself. He continued in a lethargic state for three successive days.

About twelve at night he swooned away, and became speechless for a considerable time , then raising his dim eyes to heaven, cried, ' Oh' merciful God ! receive the spirit of a penitent sinner !—Oh! Emma—Oh! Charlotte —pray for me—I am going ''— then closed his eyes in endless night, and expired. May his crimes be blotted out!

I immediately sent for Mrs. Harris, Charlotte and I were incapable of giving any necessary orders, fatigue of body and mind had so overpowered us.

Harris gave all directions concerning the funeral, and his remains were laid by those of his mother

He bequeathed his estate to Charlotte and me, with a thousand pounds to his sister Harriet, who was then out of the kingdom with her husband.

Henry Courtney was too delicate to hint his wishes to Charlotte at the present time, and, soon after the funeral, took his leave of us for a while Williams and his Matilda we could not part with, and, instead of the sum of money which was promised, we made it double, and Harris let him a farm, which he stocked, and managed our business and his own with the greatest attention.

The scene of death we had been witness to so recently, much depressed our spirits, and impaired our health, we thought it best to change the place of our abode, and go for some time to Hammond Castle, which was now become our own. We had every thing that affluence could bestow, yet, without Edwin, it could not give perfect ease, no, not for one day. When we arrived at the castle, I found myself even more depressed, if possible, every spot served but to remind me of him. The old oak, whose luxuriant shades served to cover me in my infant state, was often frequented by me, and hallowed in my imagination with a kind of enthusiasm. I had a new and most romantic walk made through the grove, which led to it from the house, and planted a shrubbery near it, with a variety of all the most beautiful flowering shrubs that nature could bestow. It soon became one of the most beautiful parts of the whole demesne

We had not been many weeks at the castle, when our male friends came to join us Mrs. Fortescue would have made one of the party, but expected to be soon confined. The friend of Edwin accompanied them, and Charlotte seemed much embarrassed at his arrival. I knew she loved him, and thought it too great a sacrifice to make to friendship, to deprive herself of so va-

luable a companion for my sake. I urged
her, in vain, to listen to his addresses,
' No, my Emma, I cannot part with you:
well as I love Henry Courtney, still you
are dearer to me' Why did he come to
disturb our present tranquillity?"

Harris and my brother were all gaiety;
we returned a few visits made by some of
the nobility in the neighbourhood, which
we had deferred till our gentlemen should
arrive, and were now obliged to give
entertainments, which we had but little
relish for, retirement being alone most cordial to our feelings however, lest singula-
rity should be carried too far, we complied
sometimes with the customs of society.

I have observed through life, that it is
better to avoid, as much as possible, the
rust of particularities, yet, those oppressed
with uncommon trials, and who have the
most exquisite sensibility, seldom hit that
medium I found that Charlotte, in all
our parties of social delight, shunned every
occasion of giving Henry the smallest opportunity of paying particular attention to

her, in consequence of which he became pensive. Though Henry was the first and only attachment Charlotte ever knew, yet, strange to tell, she positively declared against a change in her situation; though the man of her choice solicited her hand, in every look and action. I wished from my soul that this union might take place, I saw happiness to my friend await it. Henry was the chosen and beloved of Edwin to no other man on earth could I resign my Charlotte he alone I thought was worthy of possessing her. She was an invaluable treasure to me, my all that was left to make life desirable, yet, to Henry I could resign her. I hinted my wishes to Charlotte, and told her, it need not cause a total separation between us, but I could get no satisfactory answer.

About a fortnight after my brother's arrival at the castle, an account came that his lady was taken ill, and we were all too solicitous about the event to stay behind him. Accordingly we set off immediately, Charlotte and I having engaged our-

selves as sponsors ; besides, our presence
was absolutely necessary on other occasions.
On our arrival, my brother met us with all
the transport becoming the father of a
lovely girl. I eagerly caressed this new
little relation , she became a fresh tie to my
heart, and I felt comfort every time I took
the babe in my arms We gave her my
mother's name, and prayed to Heaven she
might inherit her virtues.

I set out again for Hammond Castle, and
got a promise from my brother and his family, that they would follow us very shortly ' You have now a double inducement,'
said I. ' None is necessary, where my Emma is,' replied my affectionate brother. I
desired him to bring Henry Courtney with
him, unknown to Charlotte. Henry was
deserving a better fate than to be rejected
by her , partial as I was, yet I could think
him deserving of her, and he alone — I
knew he was possessed of virtue and honour,
or Edwin would not have loved him. My
friends came in about a month after we left
them, with the lover of Charlotte, Harris,

his mother, and sisters, and, I may venture to say, a more affectionate group of friends never were collected in one house.—Reading, music, and conversation, filled the vacant hours, not engaged by visitors those of our neighbourhood were not much adapted to our taste, and we were never so truly happy as in the bosom of our own family. In the midst of friends, I made a practice of spending an hour in meditation and prayer, on my favourite improved spot, which I have already described. There were many such all through the improvements ; but none so much frequented by me. Edwin's old spaniel was still alive, and generally my attendant in my rambles.

It was in the delightful month of June, and the sun in its full meridian, when I betook me to my shade, and left Charlotte with the rest of the females at their music. The gentlemen all gone on a fishing party, and my brother's daughter, the little Eliza, lay smiling in her sleep, like an angel of innocence.

I had not been in my solitude more than
a quarter of an hour, when I perceived the
old spaniel bounding with uncommon ac-
tivity, he would run to and from me, as he
was grown stupid with age, I remarked him
the more, for the extacy he showed, and
naturally concluded some of the family
had found me out, and were approaching I
came forth from the shade, and stood on
the walk which led to the house. that I
might see what animated the poor old dog
I espied a man at a small distance—I
gazed with eager eyes—Was it Edwin?
—No—but it was his faithful Thomas,
had it been Edwin I could scarcely have
been more astonished —I was seized with
terror, and burst into tears. The poor fellow, throwing himself on his knees, declared he did not wish to frighten me.—
' Oh ' Thomas,' said I, ' it is no wonder that I am alarmed—where have you
been ?' The dog intruded again, and
threw him flat on his face with one jump
he made at Thomas—' Where have you
been, Thomas?' said I.—' With my master,

madam.'——' Your master, Thomas!'—
' Yes, madam ' ' You were with him,
no doubt, while he was alive—but since—'
' Indeed, my good lady, I was with him dead
and alive and, if you will have a little
patience, I will tell you something. I was
sent before to prevent the too sudden
emotions of joy —for joy awaits you, my
lady !' ' Merciful powers!' said I, ' then
does Edwin live?' Here Thomas again
paused ——Oh ! ye souls, who ever knew
the power, or felt the passion of love, to
you I appeal, and you alone can judge of
my heart, when, after many pauses—' *He
does live!*' vibrated in my ear. ' And
where is he, Thomas? shall I behold him
again?' ' Oh ! miss, he is not very far off,
and only sent me to prepare all his friends,
particularly you for his arrival, that he
might not alarm you too much' ' If
that be true, Thomas,' said I, why did
he not write?' ' Why, as to that, madam,
I can't say, but I did as he bade me.'
Thomas kept eagerly looking about him —
' Now, my good miss, if you will but

compose yourself,' said he, ' and sit down again in the shade, I shall only be a short time away, and will return again with more tidings to you, but you must promise not to be so disturbed · it was for that I came before, to avoid frightening you.' ' Came before whom, Thomas?— where is your master?' ' Oh ! that I will tell you by and by, if you will but have patience till I return—it shan't be long.' ' Well, do my good man,' said I, ' and I shall endeavour to collect myself for the event :'—Thomas left me. When alone, I threw myself on my knees, and with uplifted hands and eyes, poured out, in the fulness of my soul, praise and thanksgiving to the great author of all events !

Thomas returned just as I rose to retire, and delivered me a note, written with a pencil, in the well-known hand of Edwin.

' My beloved Emma, I only wish to prepare the way before I appear, lest the too sudden shock might overpower you, and the rest of my friends.—Be composed,

‘ Thy own, thy long-lost Edwin's here,
‘ Restor'd to love and thee.’

I had scarcely finished reading this note, when he clasped me in his arms, and pressed me to his heart. ‘ Have I found you again, my Emma? and in the very spot your infant cries first melted my soul to compassion.’ We looked, we gazed unutterable joy. Poor Thomas wept with his master and I, nor was the old dog an insensible spectator, for he knew, and fawned upon his master.

Edwin looked with delight at the improvements I had made around the old oak, and whispered me, ‘ in this spot our hands shall be joined.’ ‘ How will you acquaint our friends?’—‘ I shall leave the entire management of it to you,’ said I: ‘ if you had come suddenly, I do not know what the consequence might have been. I fear for Charlotte's surprise, and wish it was over with her I do not think she will bear it as well as I. What shall we do?—it is best to send Thomas to prepare the way.’ ‘ By all means,’ said he, ‘ let

him just act as he did by you ' The word
was only passed his lips, when we heard
their voices, and Charlotte say , ' I warrant
she is in her retreat—one might imagine
some favourite swain attends her there '
On looking in, and calling Emma, she
got a glimpse of her dear long-lost brother ,
a loud scream followed, and she swooned
away ' Oh ' now the worst is over,' said
I,' and rested her head on my lap, while
Edwin restored her to life with his caresses.
' Oh ' where am I ?' said the dear affrighted
girl—I saw my brother's ghost '—dear
gentle spirit, where are you gone ?' ' Here,
my Charlotte,' said he, ' alive, and come
again never to part till death !' ' How
came this to pass ?—Dead and alive ' Oh '
it is too much.' ' Be composed, and in a
little time I will unfold the mystery of
my long concealment—it was unavoidable '
' I am more than blessed,' said she, ' once
more to fold thee thus to my heart And
is it then real !' looking steadfastly in his
face, ' it is my Edwin ' but he is much al-
tered. ' Long confinement,' replied he,

' has changed my looks, but I shall soon recover, had our dear parents lived to partake this meeting, I had been doubly blest '

The two Miss Harrises were silent spectators of this affecting scene, and Thomas was sent to the house, to prepare the rest of our friends for the reception of Edwin. With fluttering hearts and feeble knees, Charlotte and I each took an arm of Edwin, and our tears flowed fast. As we had a quarter of a mile to walk to the house, weakness obliged us to sit a few moments to recover. I perceived Edwin's expressive features glow with rapture, as he passed his well-known and favourite walks. I asked him why he came so abruptly, after sending his little note. ' I was then,' said he, ' in the thickest part of the wood, and could not resist the impulse of following Thomas, when he told me where you were. I left my horses at the inn, and had walked the last six miles of my journey, on purpose to lay a plan of disguise for coming to the house, but Thomas, finding you in your retreat, frustrated my scheme. it is now many months since my departure, and a tedious confinement I have had, separated from all that made life desirable ' He was going to proceed with some account of his secreting himself so long, when my brother and sister, Courtney, and Harris, with the mother of the latter, leaning on the arm of her son, came full in our view. Henry was the first to spring forward to embrace his friend, and each received him with exulting transport. By the time we reached the house, the hall was filled with all the old domestics and tenants of the family, and nothing but general joy resounded within the gates of Hammond Castle

A tent was pitched next day, for the purpose of dining all the poor on the estate, and music for the young, to welcome home their master. A month glided away unperceived, friends, mirth, and music, all our hours employed. Edwin gave us a

short narrative of his pretended death, he
did not wish to relate it at all, it hurt his
feelings too much, to mention the inhu-
manity of a brother, who determined his
life should be the forfeit of his union with
me When he found Edwin had not died
of the wound, his confidential servant had
divulged all his future intentions in a letter to Thomas, and positively affirmed,
that a plot was formed to destroy Edwin,
if our union should take place. This man
of Lord George's advised Thomas, if he
valued the life of his master, to fly with
him to some secret place, that writing was
not safe by any means, as his master had
frequently intercepted letters, and though
great caution and secrecy was used, yet he
had found out his residence at Bath, on
which the report of his death was formed,
as the only means of assuaging the wrath of
his enemy. Lord George quitted Bath
shortly after an account of his brother's death
appeared in the public papers —' I hope my
brother's repentance was sincere,' said the
amiable Edwin, ' and now let the remem-

brance of our misfortunes and sufferings
be erased from our hearts, that no disagreeable idea may damp the remainder of our
lives , and may joy and peace close the end of
thy days and mine,' turning round to me,
and taking my hand. I cast a look at Henry,
and perceived his eyes fixed on Charlotte, as
if he were from his soul echoing to the words
of Edwin.

Henry had applied to me to be his advo-
cate, and I resigned it to my lover, as a
more powerful one, together with my right
and title to the estate of Hammond Castle,
bequeathed me by the late Lord George
Edwin's reply to this offer was , 'It is needless to contend about who shall possess it,
as I hope our interests will be one, but perhaps I am mistaken, women are liable to
change , perhaps, after all my sufferings, I
may be rejected ' This speech pierced my
heart I believe it was the only one that ever
fell from his lips, that hurt my feelings I
was obliged to retire Charlotte came
to me, and shortly after Edwin himself ,
making it a request, that she would not

leave the room, as he had something to communicate to her. ‘ Have I undesignedly offended you, Emma ? I only said, women were liable to change. Had I thought you were one of those women, I should never have placed my affections on you.’ ‘ And dearly have you suffered for so doing,’ said I, ‘ I should not wonder, Sir, if you should wish to change   you have had nothing but disagreeable circumstances attending your attachment to me — some of a most extraordinary nature.   I am more than thankful to Providence that your life was not the sacrifice ,— and I now, in the presence of your sister, free you from any obligation of uniting yourself to me, lest that train of misfortunes, which has hitherto followed us, might still attend it   ‘ Oh ! madam, I see but too plainly that I am rejected, and shall act accordingly ’   He was quitting the room hastily, but Charlotte caught hold of him —‘ Stay, my brother. you are both determined to be hasty to-day —these little quarrels love must needs forgive. Come, be in a good humour with each other.—One is as necessary to the other's happiness as their existence what need then of these jealousies?—Fix on a time, and join those hands whose hearts have been so long united.'——' And will you, Charlotte,' returned he, ' consent to become the wife of my friend?—He has long loved you, and is alone deserving of you;—let one day unite us '—As the words *I will* passed the lips of Charlotte, Edwin pressed mine to his, and then we returned to the company, in a better humour than we had left them. Edwin called Henry to walk, and made him acquainted with his happiness. Our friends talked of leaving us but their stay was necessary a few days longer.

It was our custom often to dine out in different parts of the improvements, sometimes on the grass, and at others in a temple surrounded by a river, most beautiful by nature and art It ran in a winding course, and the banks were ornamented with wild shrubs, violets, primroses, and a profusion of all that made nature lovely, beside the melody of the birds, echoing through the grove. The heart must be cold, indeed, that such a view would not warm to adore the great Lord of all.

Our family were to dine in the temple, and dinner waited a considerable time for the gentlemen, who were absent, while we amused ourselves in this enchanting place, their arrival was at last announced, and with them Mr. Welldone Neither Charlotte nor I ever once imagined that any thing extraordinary would take place on that day, and supposed the parson was come to take a family dinner, which being ended, one of the Miss Harrises told me archly, she hoped for the honour of being my bride-maid the other sister made the same speech to Charlotte. Young Harris gave the whisper to his mother, and she, rising from table, was followed by Edwin and Courtney, and thus, without fixing on a day, or making any parade whatever, we were surprised with a double wedding Edwin took my hand, and Courtney that of his Charlotte, and led us on to her favourite old oak, a romantic thought of

Edwin's, to have us joined under it he had not even a ring to provide, having the same still that was got for the former occasion Edwin offered his sister first, but Henry would not be first married 'This is useless form,' said the parson, ' please to come forwards ' At these words, as he addressed them to Edwin, my heart rose as if it would have flown out of its cell, and the ceremony began I could scarcely support myself through it, though the chosen of my soul was made mine for ever! Charlotte felt the same emotions, though she seemed to get through the ceremony better

As we returned to the temple. Mrs. Harris told us, that she took upon herself the management of the wedding, and hoped each party would be pleased, for she looked on the preparations for such occasions as really irksome, and would much annoy such delicate minds We thanked her heartily for her little plan. and assured her we were grateful to her, for having saved us all the parade of a public wedding

To prevent the intrusion of visitors, we

settled matters so as to return to town with
our friends Our little favourite, Eliza,
grew apace, and it was agreed on by all parties, that she should be left behind indeed,
had it not been for the apprehension of the in-
trusions of persons in the neighbourhood,
most of whom were not much esteemed by any
of our family, I should much rather have remained in the quiet shades of Hammond
Castle.

Mrs. Fortescue and I embraced our darling little Eliza, and, followed by our faithful old Thomas, our carriage was the last
in procession We took the road to our
late almost-deserted home, and found Matilda and Williams in raptures of joy and
gratitude. I took Matilda with me to town
where we all arrived safe, and a happier
group never entered that great metropolis

My Edwin began to regain his natural
bloom, and, though older than I by fifteen
years, yet the disparity was scarcely visible.
Henry and Charlotte consented, at our mutual and most earnest entreaties, to remain
with us. Charlotte and I could not bear

a separation. We had spent three months in town, when Edwin, who was never fond of the bustle of public life, resolved to return to the castle Henry and he went a few days before, to prepare for our reception. and, on our arrival, a most sumptuous entertainment was prepared.

My brother, who returned with us, was delighted with his little daughter, lovely in infant smiles, who welcomed us home Edwin had a band of music to hail us as we entered the great hall, and all that love and friendship could bestow, was continually poured in blessings on us. Edwin idolised my little favourite Eliza he has often told me, she was the express image of myself when he first beheld me, but, how were his joys increased, when, in something less than a year, he became the father of a beauteous boy ! The endearing tenderness with which he treated me on this occasion, recompensed me for all my sufferings I became nurse to my little boy, and we had the blessing of seeing him thrive to our wishes

A romantic thought occurred to us both, that we should unite the little Eliza and our son, provided they liked each other when they grew up. Charlotte and Mrs Harris stood sponsors for him, and we gave him the name of Henry, a beloved one of Charlotte's and that of Edwin's father.

Our days glided on, blessed and blessing each other. Charlotte, as yet, had no child, and all her maternal affections were lavished on mine; nothing remarkable happened until our son arrived almost to maturity, except my having three children more, none of which survived their birth. The young Eliza had now attained her fourteenth year; her stature, like her features, was formed with the most exact symmetry; a thousand beauties played round her mouth—her eyes beamed with sensibility and spirit, and her hair, which was uncommonly long, hung over her shoulders in all the wild negligence of nature; her young companion, Henry, not less beautiful, showed the first emotions of sorrow at being separated from her, his playfellow her mother taking her home for some time

Our poor Henry grew melancholy, and all his little sports were forgotten. His indulgent father tried every means to divert him, but in vain. ' Bring me back Eliza,' he would say, ' I have no one here to play with ' We told him he should shortly go to school, and have a number of little boys to amuse him. ' Oh! that won't do—I I can't do without Eliza—if you send her with me, I will go any where you please.' I hugged the dear boy to my heart, while a tear stood in the eye of his father. ' You shall go to your Eliza, my darling,' said I , ' she cannot come to you for some time.' His young heart was cheered at the idea, and his father and I prepared next day to indulge our boy with a visit to his young friend. Their meeting was beyond any thing conceivable of affection, Eliza's was not less, but she disguised it better than Henry. On our arrival, her cheeks glowed with crimson, and when Henry embraced

her in his arms, she burst into tears. ' Do
you cry because I came to see you, Eliza?'
said Henry ' No,' answered Eliza, ' but
I am so overjoyed to see my dear aunt !'——
' Well, it is not me, then?' said Henry,
looking disappointed. ' Upon my word,
Master Henry,' cried my brother, ' I believe
you want to coax my daughter, young as
you are.' The two children left the room
together, at a whisper between them, and I
took that opportunity of telling my brother
and sister how poor Henry grieved for his
little companion. When their son came
from school, they said they were sure he
would be much happier with him when they
got acquainted, and he was expected in a
few days.

Edwin and I were called home sooner
than we intended, by a letter from Courtney, informing us that our dear Charlotte
was taken dangerously ill, and, leaving our
boy behind us, we flew to my dear and beloved friend ; we found her ill in the extreme, her disorder terminating in a fever
of the most dangerous kind her fond and

tender Henry watched continually round her sick bed, and I prevailed on Edwin to return to London, to preserve him from the danger of infection. It was the first time we ever separated for a week since our marriage, and the only cause for a sigh during that period, was the illness of my friend; but perfect happiness is not always to be the lot of mortals · my Charlotte, on the fifteenth day after her illness, expired in my arms, leaving a fond husband and her friend for ever to mourn her loss.

She left no child to inherit her many virtues. This trial had nearly broken my heart: Edwin returned, and used all his efforts to console his friend. It was, I think, to me like the separation of soul and body, when I saw my long-loved friend taken out to be interred · the funeral was attended by a vast number of people of every description, her benevolent heart rendered her beloved by all.——Mrs Harris, her son, and daughters, came to comfort me, and we had Eliza and Henry brought home to amuse us.

Time alone could reconcile me to this fatal loss —My Edwin feared lest my health should be the forfeit of my unavailing sorrow, and, notwithstanding all his tenderness, and kindest soothings to assuage my melancholy, the pale cheek of my Charlotte, lovely even in death, was still fresh in my recollection.

No human happiness can remain perfect for a long duration, as mine was from my union with Edwin till this fatal stroke in the loss of my friend.—Friendship, thou all refining touch of Heaven! thy kindling emulation ever gives a self-actuating goodness, to vulgar minds unknown

We had the satisfaction to see our Henry and his fair companion grow in beauty, grace, and mutual tenderness. The most earnest wish of our hearts was, to see them united, and, as age was now stealing on apace, to leave those beloved objects to inherit our large possessions. Henry had now attained his two-and-twentieth year, and was so enamoured of his lovely Eliza, that he applied to his uncle and aunt for their consent. The hearts and hands of our children were joined, and all the festivity of the occasion duly attended to They were in possession of all that joy, love, and opulence could bestow The virtues of his father were emulated by our Henry, and he never was the occasion of a sigh to me.

Thus was I amply repaid by Heaven, in blessings, for a life begun in sorrow—a foundling in a wood. By never swerving from the paths of virtue, I have attained perhaps more of the real felicity of life than commonly falls to the lot of mortals.

THE END.

J. Swan, Printer, Angel street, Newgate Street, London

Just published,

THE
SATIRICAL VIEW OF LONDON,
For the Year 1803, in 1 vol. 12mo.
By JOHN CORRY

———

THE
THREE MONKS!!!
Two vols. translated from the French

———

LINDORF AND CAROLINE,
OR THE
DANGER OF CREDULITY
Three vols. A Cabalistical Romance, translated
from the German of Professor Kramer, Author
of Herman of Unna.

———

ALFRED BERKLEY,
OR THE
DANGERS OF DISSIPATION
By JOHN CORRY.

Lightning Source UK Ltd.
Milton Keynes UK
UKHW022014190820
368517UK00011B/256

9 781375 082617